The gifts depend on the natural world
and are intricately and luminously linked
to the universe.

SHARE *the* INHERITANCE

*We must recognise that we have a great treasure to guard;
that the inheritance in our possession represents
the prolonged achievement of the centuries....*

−Winston Churchill

SHARE *the* INHERITANCE

Gifts of Intangible and Tangible Wealth

Catherine Glass and David Abbott

THE INHERITANCE PRESS

Credits for the images and quotations appear according to page number in the Notes, which begin on Page 123.

Printed in the United Kingdom

Butler Tanner & Dennis
Caxton Road, Frome, Somerset

ISBN 978-0-9843921-0-0

THE INHERITANCE PRESS

Lake Oswego, Oregon, United States
Shawford, Hampshire, United Kingdom

DEDICATION

This book is dedicated to our children and grandchildren and to children everywhere.

PATRONS & SUPPORTERS

We are very grateful to the Patrons & Supporters whose contributions and assistance have helped us to share the Inheritance:

JAMES BAXENDALE, ESQUIRE

KATERINA EYRE BREWER

MARTIN HASLAM

JILL KIRK NOTTAGE

CHARANJIV S PARMAR, *whose support is given in recognition that, 'Even Kings and emperors with heaps of wealth and vast dominions cannot compare with an ant filled with the love of God'.*

LORD PEARSON OF RANNOCH

LES AND PAULA SMITH

Contents

ACKNOWLEDGEMENTS

DESIGN
Christine Ambrose and Catherine Glass

IMAGE RESEARCH
Catherine Glass

LAYOUT
Christine Ambrose

COMPOSITE IMAGES
Christine Ambrose

CARTOONS
Lena Lenček

TITLE DESIGN
Susan Muther
susan@breedworks.biz

RESEARCH ASSISTANCE & PROOFREADING
John Petley
johnpetley@yahoo.co.uk

Foreword

By the Baroness Cox of Queensbury

Test everything. Hold fast to what is good.
—1 Thessalonians 5:21

Men and women co-created 'The Inheritance'. They lived with love, courage, laughter and wisdom, and the gifts they gave were so rich they gave life to others for hundreds of years. Some of those men and women appear in *Share the Inheritance.*

On my journeys behind the Iron Curtain and to war zones in Sudan, Burma and Nagorno Karabakh, I have met many people who were denied the gifts of the Inheritance. As a result they were very vulnerable. Many were in danger of losing their lives, and they were deeply concerned for the future of their children.

In 'The West' we have become subject to the influence of aggressive secular humanism and extreme relativism, reflected in 'politically correct multiculturalism' and in a loss of appreciation of anything which is good in our cultural, political and spiritual heritage. Many people therefore have lost any sense of vision—and 'without a vision, the people perish'.

There is, therefore, an urgent need to recreate a vision, which will preserve all that is best in our heritage.

Share the Inheritance invokes that vision. It is old. It is new. It is 'a condition of complete simplicity'. It is a challenging book, which will inspire thought and suggest plans of action for healing and rebuilding both individuals and societies.

The motto of the Royal Society is *Nullius in verba*—'Take nobody's word for it'. Don't take my word for it. Read *Share the Inheritance, Gifts of Intangible and Tangible Wealth* for yourself and come to your own conclusions.

BARONESS CAROLINE COX, a life peer in the House of Lords, has been 'a voice for the voiceless' for decades. She made multiple trips behind the Iron Curtain to help the Polish people's struggle for freedom. In thanks, they awarded her the Commander Cross of the Order of Merit. She made sixty-nine journeys to Armenia to learn the truth about the conflict in Nagorno Karabakh and to bring medical supplies to the wounded. In thanks, Armenia awarded her the Mikhitar Gosh Medal. The author of *The Rape of Reason*, Caroline Cox was founder and Chancellor of the University of Bournemouth and is currently Chancellor of Liverpool Hope University. A recipient of the William Wilberforce Award, she is the founder-CEO of the Humanitarian Aid Relief Trust (HART), which sponsors a programme that heightens awareness of existing problems, identifies solutions and empowers oppressed peoples.

A Note from David and Catherine...

AT FIRST we didn't grasp how valuable our shared Inheritance is. David had spent decades diagnosing illness and prescribing cures when he began to realize the connection between infirmity, malaise and disease and the loss of the Inheritance. Catherine was affected by the misery of the people of Communist Prague when she visited her grandmother there before the Velvet Revolution. Searching for the missing source of healing and wholeness for ourselves and for others, we began to see, dimly at first, the Inheritance.

Slowly, we became aware of the men and women who had helped to create the Inheritance—men and women who saw clearly, loved passionately and acted courageously. They showed us that the Inheritance is an extraordinary source of happiness and prosperity, justice and creativity, compassion, character formation and transformation.

We looked for a history that illuminated the gifts of the Inheritance. When we couldn't find what we needed, we created the book you hold in your hands.

You may find our book eccentric because we focus on gifts helped into existence by the people of the British Isles and their diaspora. This is not the whole story of the Inheritance—many people have helped to create the Inheritance in other parts of the world. It is the part of the story that we know, a personal account, which we hope resonates with you.

Oscar Wilde observed that a cynic is *a man who knows the price of everything and the value of nothing*. In contrast, you know the value of many things and are likely to know far more than we have been able to include here. You will examine the Inheritance we've described with your experience and vision thereby deepening and enlarging this account.

We've come to believe that the Inheritance forms a life-giving ring and that with the loss of even one gift, the circle is broken. Fortunately, as this history shows, the more the Inheritance is shared, the richer it grows.

GIFT 1

Stonehenge is the most famous of Megalithic monuments. Megalithic builders were searching for the first gift.

THE ANCESTORS of the people who created the Inheritance were the ancestors of us all. Their descendants had come and gone in Europe and the northern islands, retreating as mile-thick ice advanced, returning as the ice melted.

Thousands of years ago they left their sanctuaries in the south to hunt mammoths and reindeer across northern European tundra. At times the English Channel was a dry rift valley. Hunters crossed the valley on foot. Eight thousand years ago, rising waters again swept through the valley, flooding the plains that now lie under the Irish and North Seas and creating islands. Six thousand years ago, Megalithic people began raising great rings of stone on the islands.

I am a part of all that I have met;
Yet all experience is an arch
*   wherethro'*
Gleams that untravell'd world,
*   whose margin fades*
For ever and for ever
*   when I move.*

*   —Alfred Lord Tennyson*

Megalithic people hunted salmon, pig and deer. Life could be short and harsh, but they did not retreat from reality. They tried to meet adversity, just as you do. They looked for ways of understanding their world.

The Ring of Brodgar

Archaeologists, mathematicians and astronomers have suggested that Megalithic people had different reasons for building their henges—colossal rings of stone with earthworks and ditches. A cosmic explanation takes into account the henges, their great processional avenues and the prehistoric landscape around them. Astronomers observed that the henges and avenues were aligned with the rising and setting Sun of the Summer and Winter Solstices, and that distant knolls on the horizon may have been used as 'foresights' to study the Moon. They suggest that the henges were *astronomical clocks*.

Megalithic people may not have created 'clocks' in stone, but they clearly identified recurring lunar and solar events that were crucial to their lives, including their early forays into agriculture. They memorialized their knowledge and their hopes in the henges. They were among the first people to seek a gift that will be fundamental to science and to our lives.

During the Bronze Age, the people of the islands tamed wolves, raised horses and cattle in lush pastures, sailed ships and traded in tools, gold, silver and pearls. They expanded their knowledge of the hidden source of life buried in the earth. They learned to plant, harvest and nurture crops and to make bread and beer. They went hungry if necessary to preserve seed for the next planting. They, too, were seeking the gift.

Out of the first gift comes the understanding that vegetable life rises out of a seed buried in the dark earth.

'What I saw far surpassed my wildest dreams.' Early in the 20th century, the first pilots flying above England observed ghostly lines in country fields. Archaeologists discovered they were the pale traces of prehistoric buried towns, droveways and waterways.

You can appreciate that if the first gift is unknown or neglected, science and invention fail to thrive. If it is invested, we receive enormous benefits.

GIFT 1

The Earth and the Universe Follow Laws which Affect Us and These Laws Can Be Described and Predicted.

The people who lived two thousand years ago on the islands valued this gift. But they knew that they and their children had to possess the second gift if they were going to have any chance for happiness.

GIFT 2

Created in the 1st century BC, the Great Torc from the Snettisham Hoard floats above Eggardon Hill, an Iron Age fort in Dorset. Cloaked by windswept grass, the islands' hill forts and fields still guard chariot fittings, shields, swords, jewels and gold necklaces.

TO BE forbidden to choose your friends or your job, to be unable to live where you like, travel freely or eat when you are hungry—all this resembles slavery; but to be a slave is far worse, and the people of the islands knew it.

They knew that to be a slave meant you worked without pay. Your master owned everything you had earned. You could not protect yourself or those you loved. You could not drink a glass of water or step into the shade if your master forbade you. They feared that if they were conquered, they would become slaves.

**The words FREE and FRIEND
share the same root.**

The island peoples wanted to be free, and they wanted their friends to be free. When they used the word free about a person, they meant that person was dear to them.

Over the centuries, behind the defensive moat of the English Channel and the sea, they had held invaders at bay. They fought off the Romans in 55 BC. In AD 43, the Romans returned, this time with cavalry and elephants.

The people of the islands decided to fight the invaders. This might not be what you would choose to do, since to fight means to risk death, but it was the choice they made.

Old epics tell us that Iron Age people laughed and loved, were hospitable and brave, and cherished their children.

By 1000 BC, speakers of English had dropped case endings, which tell how a word is being used in a sentence. Streamlined, English began welcoming foreign words and today has the world's largest vocabulary.

❀

In 1776, Washington would recall the words of Calgacus—

Remember, officers and soldiers, that you are Freemen, fighting for the blessings of liberty; that slavery will be your portion, and that of your posterity, if you do not acquit yourselves like men.

❀

Like the people of the islands, the Athenians had fought to defend their country against the overwhelming might of an empire. They defeated a massive host of invaders in 490 BC. Ten years later, the invaders were back. Vastly outnumbered, the Greeks united to resist them. At the Battle of Salamis they sailed toward the invaders shouting,

> *Eleutheria, Eleutheria!*
> *Freedom! Freedom!*

Without their courage, Socrates, Euripedes, Plato and our modern world would never have been.

They fought the Romans on the beaches and in the fields and in the hills. They fought them on the Thames and in the west and in the north. The men and women of the islands fought for their freedom against the Romans for more than 150 years.

Sometime around AD 83, the legions marched north toward present-day Scotland. Calgacus, chieftain of the Caledonians, and his men made a last stand. Before they went into battle Calgacus told them—

> *The Romans make a wasteland and call it peace.*
>
> *. . . Our brothers and sons are torn from us by conscription to be slaves. . . .*
>
> *As you advance into battle, think of your fathers and your children!*

Calgacus and his men fought to the bitter end. *The next day, an awful silence reigned.*

But this was not the end.

Marking the northern limit of Roman control, Hadrian's Wall ran 73 and a half miles from the River Tyne to Solway Firth. Built by Roman legions and completed in AD 136, the huge wall included stone and turf, forts and ditches.

Bristling with forts and Roman soldiers, Hadrian's Wall was meant to isolate the islanders of the north who had not surrendered. But they would not stay put. They broke through the wall, and when a second wall was built, they broke through that.

They never forgot that they loved freedom. Over the next two thousand years the islanders would face invaders at least fifteen times. They and other peoples of the Earth helped to create a foundational bequest—

GIFT 2
To Live Fully, Men and Women Must Refuse to be Conquered and Must Affirm Their Independence.

London children outside their bombed home. Men and women fought to protect them from Nazi invasion.

GIFT 3

A HAPPY CIVILIZATION depends on the third gift. Emblematic stories about it have been told in different cultures and places, including the islands.

In the forest and meadows of the islands in the third century, Roman civilization appeared to be advanced—Roman laws were carved in stone, two thousand miles of Roman roads crossed Britain, Roman villas had hypocaust heating—hot water pipes under the floors. But as burial evidence makes appallingly clear, babies, teenagers and the physically handicapped were sacrificed to appease imaginary gods and demons. In the Roman city of Verulamium, archaeologists have found the heads of battered victims displayed on temple poles.

It was in this city that Alban lived, probably in the 4th century. He will have to answer one question—*Will you risk your life to save your friend?*

Waves of persecutions swept across the Roman Empire. A friend could mean the difference between life and death, but which of your friends could you trust?

> *There is a disease that is always part of tyranny—never to be able to trust a friend.*
>
> *–Aeschylus*

Roman soldiers ruthlessly hunted the followers of Christ, who opposed the horror of human sacrifice, and refused to worship the Emperor. A Christian, a friend of Alban's, asked him for shelter.

Despite the risk, Alban took him in. Eventually Romans arrived to search Alban's house. Like the man who throws himself on a live grenade to save others, Alban put on his friend's cloak, and handed himself over in his place. The Romans arrested him. His friend escaped.

Alban was taken to the governor. In response to interrogation, Alban stunned him by saying—

> *I worship and adore the true and living God who created all things.*

The governor ordered him scourged. Alban refused to worship Caesar and renounce Christ. The governor ordered him beheaded.

Roman soldiers took Alban outside the city walls and across the river. A crowd of people followed. They saw radiance brighter than sunlight in his face, and believed it was a *charism*—a gift from God.

Roman walls and the Cathedral and Abbey Church of St Alban

At the top of a grassy hill, Alban faced his executioner. The executioner looked into Alban's face, and refused to behead him. *No*, he said, when ordered. *No*.

On the hill where the Abbey and Cathedral church now stand, Romans beheaded both Alban and the executioner who had refused to kill him.

Alban gave his life for a gift precious to us—

GIFT 3
Friendship, a Dear, Life-enhancing Gift that Springs from Selfless Love and is Grounded in Equality—a True Friend is Always an Equal.

...within every human person is an inviolable haven, a free space, where state power may not tread—and that acknowledgement is the beginning of limited government and freedom of conscience.

—George Weigel

Greater love hath no man than this—that he lay down his life for his friends.

—Jesus

The legends that people remember tell us what matters to them.

GIFT 4

THE NAME of the executioner who refused to execute has been forgotten, but he inaugurated an exceptional bequest, on which justice and human dignity depend—

I wonder if we realize just how precious this spirit of friendliness and kindness is.

—King George VI

GIFT 4
The Refusal to Obey an Unjust Order.

GIFTS 5 & 6

ONLY STEADY HANDS could protect life as the Roman Empire slowly and violently fell. Patrick seemed an unlikely candidate for this mission, but then so did Brigid, Colum Cille and Aidan.

Patrick was the saint of second chances. Kidnapped from Britain when he was a teenager, early in the 5th century, enslaved in Ireland, he was hungry and terrified for six years. Recalling in desperation the God he had abandoned, he prayed, and heard God tell him to walk away from servitude. Easier said than done, but he made a miraculous escape, and caught a boat to Roman Gaul, only to find the country devastated by invaders.

Patrick slogged his way to the monastery of St Honorat in the Mediterranean. He was middle-aged when he dreamed that the Irish were asking him to risk slavery and return to Ireland. Patrick made the long journey back. He brought news of the God called Isu Mac De, planted communities of justice and peace, and, it is said, inspired Brigid.

Brigid left the father who had tried to sell her into slavery and went to live under the oaks of Kildare. Men and women joined her. They built a community that delighted in the natural world. They taught children, nursed the sick and welcomed travellers. The music of harps filled the air. Around the time that Brigid died, in AD 521, Colum Cille was born.

After the fall of Rome, it was the Church that kept alive the vital skills of agriculture, letters, the law...

—Hugh Johnson

*But now they drift
on the still water,
Mysterious, beautiful...*

—William Butler Yeats

Colum Cille, also known as Columba, landed at Iona, an island of white sands, pink granite and thundering seas, off the west coast of Scotland.

Inspired by the communities established by Brigid and Patrick and by his love of books—he argued the first

Cloisters at Iona

Legend says that Colum Cille's mistake was to urge other men into battle to avenge an injustice. Afterward, he bitterly repented the deaths he had caused.

copyright case—Colum Cille began his real work after he made a horrific mistake. Grief stricken, he sailed into exile.

On Iona, Colum Cille tried to make amends. He curbed his fierce temper. He and twelve companions built a monastery with an oratory, sanctuary and scriptorium. At a time when libraries all over the Roman Empire were being burned to the ground, Colum Cille and the brothers made copies of the works saved from destruction. They welcomed and taught students from all over the islands, and founded monasteries and libraries across Britain.

The community of Iona believed that the world was a *translucent source of mystery, revelation and redemption.* Aidan joined the community around the time that Colum Cille died, late in the 6th century.

The gold buckle unearthed in the Sutton Hoo treasure ship is a witness to murderous strife and extraordinary craftsmanship early in the 7th century.

In what is now Northumbria, men killed the king who was Oswald's father. They took his kingdom and the Sutton Hoo buckle (above). Young Oswald fled to Iona, where he was given sanctuary. There he met Aidan, a monk who could see a person's inner face.

When he became a man, Oswald returned to gangster-torn Northumbria and recovered his kingdom. He asked Aidan to bring his people the teachings of Jesus Christ, who had inspired Alban, Patrick, Brigid and Colum Cille.

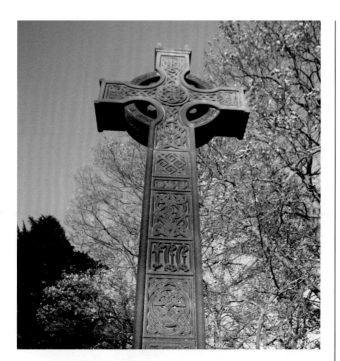

Celtic Cross in Northumbria, where Christian communities defended peace.

...the growth of personality transforms this face, which becomes gradually transparent to the moral unity that speaks and sees from it.

—Roger Scruton

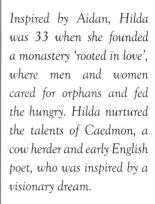

Inspired by Aidan, Hilda was 33 when she founded a monastery 'rooted in love', where men and women cared for orphans and fed the hungry. Hilda nurtured the talents of Caedmon, a cow herder and early English poet, who was inspired by a visionary dream.

Lindisfarne, an island off the coast of Northumbria, where the retreating tide opens a path to shore twice a day, became Aidan's base. He inspired Oswald's people because he could see their inner beauty and because he actually lived the teachings of Mac De. Aidan was unable to save Oswald from death in battle, but his work helped to lay the foundation for future peace.

Christian communities cared for the poor, nursed the ill, taught the young and encouraged the creativity of artists. They were grounded in a source crucial to the Inheritance.

Just as we could not describe Tibet without talking about Buddhism or Saudi Arabia without talking about Islam, we cannot describe the Inheritance without speaking about the man whom the Celts called Isu Mac De.

The radical idea that God loves justice and is merciful appeared many times in Hebrew Scripture. For instance, Psalm 89 sings —'Justice and judgment are the habitation of Thy throne: mercy and truth shall go before Thy face'.

—*Psalm 89*

Do a miracle for me, and change my heart...

—*Tadhg Óg Ó hUiginn*

Out of the Carpenter's shop at Nazareth had come a personality infinitely greater than any made by myth and legend... Born in Judea around two thousand years ago, he came as Lord and friend.

ISU IS GAELIC FOR JESUS, Mac means son and De means God. To the people of the islands Isu Mac De was the Son of God and a friend. The two conceptions—*Lord and friend*—were connected, and influenced the creation of the Inheritance in unexpected ways.

For one thing, Isu Mac De seemed to know them better than they knew themselves. He knew that they carried 'stones'. They had acquired the stones painfully—first the stones that hurt them, then the stones they thought would protect them and then the stones they threw at others.

The stones were fear, narcissism, arrogance, injustice, gluttony, envy, greed, sloth and rage. There were others. Few admitted to having the stones, but Mac De could see them. He asked them to put them down. They doubted they could.

But with Mac De's help, they did. They walked away from the stones and stood beside him—two friends facing life side by side—with a new and exhilarating confidence.

Mac De breathed cool, fresh ideas through their minds. As the New Testament records: One day while he was teaching, his mother and brothers could not reach him through the crowd, and sent him word to let them in. Those listening to Mac De thought that they were bound to defer to and elevate their blood families, and expected him to do the same.

But he looked at them and asked, *Who is my mother and who are my brothers?* And then he assured them, *Whoever does the will of God is my brother and sister and mother.* In one stroke he had dissolved the imprisoning ties of blood family, tribe and race.

He came to heal the brokenhearted, to give sight to those who cannot see and to set free those who are oppressed. He taught men and women how to live and how to love.

Asked about the man blind from birth, *Who did sin, this man or his parents that he was born blind?* Mac De said

Augustine of Canterbury and a band of monks landed on the Isle of Thanet in AD 597. The English king's response to their first sermon was—'Your words are fair, but they are new and of doubtful meaning'.

Snow falls and life grows according to fundamental principles. The principles of love give us the strength to rise and stand and live.

bluntly, *Neither*. People were not to be judged by their parents, their illness, their sex or their class.

He affirmed the value of each person, while hoping we would not stay the same. As a modern writer observed—

> God loves each of us exactly the way we are. God loves us so much He hopes we will change.

An intellectual asked him:

'What do you say is the first commandment?'

He answered:

'The Lord our God is one Lord: And you shall love the Lord your God with all your heart, and with all your soul, and with all your mind, and with all your strength; and you shall love your neighbour as yourself.'

Another thing they liked about Mac De was that he enjoyed sharing a meal. He sat down and talked and ate and drank with all those who didn't make the cut at other tables. When they were with him they felt they belonged. No one was superior to another. They were equals. They were brothers and sisters.

He knew that a man or woman needed more than food. He knew it personally. *No one lives by bread alone,* Mac De said fiercely to his antagonist in the desert, and he spoke for us. Even when we are starving, we long for more than bread.

Blessed are the peacemakers…

In the Gospels that record his words, Mac De told us that we are the sons and daughters of God. He asked us to cherish each other.

Mac De was not interested in rules for their own sake. He showed us that the only way that a person can truly love is freely—for love that is not free is not love.

He taught us to forgive each other. *How many times should I forgive a person?* Peter asked him, thinking seven times must be the outer limit. *Seventy times seven,* answered Mac De, and added, *If you forgive, then your heavenly Father will also forgive.* The disciples were stunned. As philosopher Hannah Arendt observed, *Forgiveness was a concept unknown in the ancient world until he introduced it.* Mac De understood that when we forgive those who have hurt us, we free ourselves and transform our lives. As people give and receive forgiveness, the ethos of society changes. The old revenge culture, dark with superstition, began to be overturned.

Mac De wanted leaders to serve their people. He described a new relationship between citizens and government. Gleaming with wit he held a coin inscribed with Caesar's face and said, *Pay to Caesar what belongs to Caesar.* He clearly thought that the small coin belonged to the government, while priceless things belonged to God, family and neighbours—and he wanted us to decide which was which. As a result, we might not depend on king or government to help our neighbour. We might happily help and cherish our neighbour ourselves.

One teaching fascinated them—

The Kingdom of God is within you.

He has sent me…to heal the brokenhearted…

Our Lord did not say you will never face trouble, you will never feel sorrow, you will never be afflicted—He said, 'You will not be overcome'.

— *Lady Julian of Norwich*

. . . for this I came into the world, to bear witness to the truth.

A man's life is like a sparrow's flight, an old Ealdorman told the king. It flies through the hall when you are sitting at meat in winter-tide, with the warm fire lighted on the hearth, but the icy rainstorm without. The sparrow flies in at one door and tarries for a moment in the light and heat of the hearth-fire, and then, flying forth from the other door, vanishes into the wintry darkness whence it came. So tarries for a moment the life of man in our sight, but what is before it, what after it, we know not. If this new teaching about the Son of God tells us what happens after, let us follow it.

—The Venerable Bede

'Thy kingdom come, Thy will be done, on earth as it is in heaven.'

The simple words of the Lord's Prayer reminded listeners that the source and centre of the world lay beyond government and the human race.

Second Day of Creation. Centuries of art have been inspired by Biblical teachings.

. . . receive the Holy Spirit.

Mac De showed them how to live. He promised them that their lives were eternal—and that life on Earth was only the beginning of their story.

Those who were receptive saw Him as the Creator of Heaven and Earth, the Lord of Light and a friend who had freed them from death with His death.

When they helped each other by creating charities, trusts, friendly societies, hospices, hospitals and schools, they believed He supported them. When they created a Common Law grounded in respect for the dignity and equality of every individual, they believed He cheered them. When they faced death in the cause of justice and freedom, they believed He stood with them.

He gave them two gifts that were big, beautiful and a little frightening. He seemed to think we could handle them—

GIFT 5
You Are Endowed By God with Freedom, Dignity and Responsibility.

GIFT 6
Forgiveness. People Live Better Lives When They Forgive Each Other. Their Communities Flourish.

Despots, fanatics and slave bosses have attacked these gifts, but many brave individuals, Christian and non-Christian, have defended them.

Over the centuries they also identified seven powers that would help a person live in freedom with dignity.

Look, I'm at the door, knocking. If you hear me calling and open the door, I'll come in and share your meal, side by side with you.

The greatest gift that God in His bounty made—the most reflective of His goodness and that which He prizes the most in all creation—was free will.

—Dante

The original meaning of the word responsible is to be able to respond.

Like our two hands, freedom and justice are connected. When freedom disappears, justice is lost. When justice goes missing, freedom is lost.

Bear in mind this one truth—no evil can come to a good man either in life or after death, and God does not neglect him.

—Socrates

The Latin word *virtu* means strength or power. Thinkers identified seven powers that help people thrive. Socrates described the fifth at his trial.

THE 7 POWERS

1 JUSTICE
Be fair. Speak the truth. Defend just law.

2 PRUDENCE
Build your life with common sense, foresight, imagination and the wisdom of generations.

3 TEMPERANCE
Exercise self-discipline. Be flexible, open and rational.

4 FORTITUDE
Meet adversity with courage, steadfastness and humour.

5 FAITH
Trust in God.

6 HOPE
Trust that your life has meaning and is part of a bigger story.

7 LOVE

The seven powers are versatile. They can help a person build a relationship, survive a bad economy or free his country. Most of us would prefer to use these powers while free, and freedom is our birthright. It is *not* the gift of government. But freedom needs justice to exist. Who will establish and defend justice and fair play?

Men and women standing under the night sky felt connected to the cosmos, and sensed that they lived in a universe with laws. They wanted laws that would govern relations between people—laws based on universal principles of fairness and compassion.

GIFTS 7, 8 & 9

MANY PEOPLE—among them Celts, Britons and Anglo-Saxons, ancient Greeks, the Jewish prophets, the followers of Confucius, Buddhists, Persians, Romans and Native Americans—tried to create laws that would protect the innocent and punish those who stole, hurt or murdered. But the law is a double-edged sword.

Whether the law is just or unjust depends on the source of the law. When despots are the source of the law, the law is despotic. When corrupt authorities are the source of the law, the law is corrupt. When the tribe is the source of the law, justice for individuals is often stillborn.

Everywhere people asked, Can I count on the law if I am innocent? Can I bring a case against a powerful man if he seizes my land? Can I speak in my own defence and be heard?

The tribe can cast a dark shadow. Threats, bribes and violence may be used to shield tribal members who have broken the law. 'Justice' may be decided not by what is fair but by who is most powerful. Corruption and murderous blood feuds become rife. Women are owned by men and lack human rights.

Two thousand years ago in the islands, two essential things happened—the individual began to be liberated from the tribe and the dignity and accountability of every person began to be acknowledged.

Judeo-Christian ethical teachings and Celtic and Anglo-Saxon ideas of fairness empowered individuals. So did Anglo-Saxon protection of property rights, which strengthened individuals and families. Appreciation for the benefits of using reason contributed to personal liberation. Even *wergild*—monetary reparation for a crime—strengthened a person by holding him individually accountable, and thereby reduced tribal power.

All this was beneficial, but little changed until one man pulled these ideas together and added the missing pieces.

> All that is gold does not glitter,
> Not all those who wander are lost;
> The old that is strong does not wither,
> Deep roots are not reached by the frost.
> From the ashes a fire shall be woken,
> A light from the shadows shall spring;
> Renewed shall be blade that was broken,
> The crownless again shall be king.

Around AD 849, a fourth son was born to the king of Wessex. He was given the name that means *elf wisdom*, AElfred.

Alfred learned to ride, hunt and read. Even as the dark shadows of invasion fell across the kingdom, closing the doors to peace, and shutting out the light, he pored through books.

The Vikings invaded and plundered Britain and Ireland. They burned, enslaved, terrorized and murdered.

Wessex was one of the kingdoms of England. The destruction of England had begun before the Vikings attacked. Alfred wrote—

> I remember how I saw it before it was all ravaged and burned—how the churches stood around all England, filled with treasures and books and a great company of God's servants, and how little they felt the profit of the books for they could not understand them. As if the books said, our elders who held these places before us loved wisdom and through it they got wealth and left it to us. Here we may see their traces, but we cannot follow after them, and so have lost both the wealth and the wisdom because we were not willing to bend our minds to the pursuit of learning.

The kingdoms of the north fell to Viking onslaughts. Only the kingdom of Wessex remained standing, but Wessex seemed doomed.

Alfred the scholar became Alfred the warrior. In 871, at the Battle of Ashdown, he charged against the shield wall of Vikings like a boar, and defeated them. Shortly afterwards his last living brother died. The *Witan*—a gathering of powerful (and sometimes wise) men—named him king. He was 22 years old. Alfred fought nine battles that year, winning some, losing others. Desperate for peace, he settled with the Vikings, buying them off with *danegeld*.

The Vikings swore by their god Odin's 'ring'—his armlet—to uphold the peace. But like some today, a promise meant little to them. Twice Alfred paid for peace with

gold, and twice the Vikings reneged on their promise and attacked. For a third time Alfred bought peace.

The gold belonged to the people. Its loss to the Vikings meant that families had less to live on, ships were not built and towns were not fortified, leaving them open to attack. Perhaps that is why legend records that St Neot bluntly criticized Alfred. He told him that he was not serving his people and would come to a bad end.

In 878, on Twelfth Night, Alfred celebrated the last day of Christmas at his court. That night, Vikings came with fire, axe and sword.

For a third time, the Vikings had broken their word and attacked. Alfred had a life and death choice to make.

Alfred barely escaped into the woods with his family and a small band of warriors. They fled west, taking refuge in the Somerset swamps on the island of Athelney. With Alfred were his wife, their six-year old daughter, Aethelflaed, and three-year-old son, Edward.

The Vikings spread across Wessex. They raided towns and farms, killing, raping and enslaving men and women. Alfred remained hiding in his swamp. He was warned that if he and his family did not escape across

the Channel, they would be killed. He was ill—he suffered from a painful, chronic illness. More painfully,
he did not know what to do.

He sat down and thought—about what the men and
women of Wessex needed and what he owed them,
about the king he had been and the king he wanted
to be, about his family and Christ and the likelihood
of violent death.

According to legend he decided to embark on a dan-
gerous personal mission. Risking torture and death if
discovered, he disguised himself as a harpist, and entered the Viking stronghold in Chippenham. He was
there to take personal stock of the enemy he faced. He
saw the enormous strength of the Vikings, and learned
that they planned to stay. Back in the swamp, he made
his decision.

Sending his personal guard across Wessex, he asked
the farmer-warriors of the *fyrd* to meet him at Egbert's
Stone and face the Vikings in battle with him.

He was not sure how they would respond, but he had
learned the ultimate lesson—*to be a leader he had to be
willing to die for his people.*

On the appointed day in May, Alfred saw the banners
of the Wessex *fyrd* fluttering in the wind and three
thousand farmers and warriors entering the valley.
They knew they were outnumbered, but rallying behind Alfred, they marched to Ethandun prepared to
defeat the large Viking army or die in the attempt.

Alfred led them as they charged the Viking shield wall.

> *They fought for their God-given birthright,*
> *Their country to have and to hold,*
> *And not for the lust of conquest*
> *And not for the hunger of gold.*

After fierce and bloody fighting Alfred and the men of
Wessex sent the Vikings flying from the field. Two weeks

*The word authority comes
from the Latin verb augere,
which means to facilitate
growth. How often today does
authority facilitate growth?*

*Alfred believed that his
Christian faith asked him
to turn his cheek to insult.
He did not believe that his
faith asked him to turn the
cheek of an innocent child
so she could be hit a second
time—or raped or enslaved.*

Dependable and competent leadership is vital to success everywhere.

1   *Show up. Be determined and focused.*

2   *Act with courage and lead from the front.*

3   *Be grounded, listen, take advice and think. Ideas change the world.*

4   *Serve your people and earn their trust.*

5   *Be practical and manage events.*

6   *Learn from mistakes.*

7   *Make your principles crystal clear and stand behind them.*

8   *Harness the talents and control the flaws of those working with you. Give responsibility to those who can handle it, and give them credit for success.*

later they forced them to surrender. To everyone's surprise, Alfred did not kill the Vikings. He wanted to build on what they shared—their love of poetry, song and beauty and their mutual respect for courage and fortitude.

England's creative future faced daunting challenges. As Alfred saw, he had to defend his people and convert the invaders to a new way of life.

He established a network of fortified towns and rebuilt the navy. He set up *fyrd* rotations so one force of farmers and warriors was free to go on with their business while the other force was always ready if the Vikings launched new raids, which they did. With these defences in place, Alfred and his son Edward were able to defend London and Wessex. Alfred created the possibility of peace and justice with a gift that is rarely seen in the world today.

GIFT 7

A Leader Will Always Defend His or Her People and, if necessary, Will Die for Them.

Nothing a leader does will matter if he fails to keep his people safe. But peace needed more than *fyrds* and fortifications. Alfred came to understand that the life of his people depended on two other gifts. In fact, our own lives depend on these gifts.

For centuries, the ancient laws of the islands had been memorized or written on wooden wands and passed down to succeeding generations. Medieval manuscripts refer to the legendary Molmutine Laws from the pre-Christian era. In Alfred's time there were as many laws as there were earls and kings, a hodge-podge of laws that made justice elusive.

Alfred understood that civilization could not survive without law that punished the guilty and protected the

Those who knew Alfred called him *England's darling.*

9   *Make sure your people get an education.*

10 *Tell the truth, keep your promises, treat others fairly and be swift to forgive. Follow the Ten Commandments.*

11 *Know that you are responsible to a just God for your actions, and trust that God is your friend.*

12 *Don't complain. Never give up.*

The dependable and fair rule of law, which is not changeable in mid-stream to benefit the rich or powerful, has been an ideal for millennia.

innocent. He grasped the simple fact that his people, who included Britons, Celts, Anglo-Saxons and Danes, would respect a law that was fair, grounded in honesty and common sense and easy to understand. Taking the best of their laws, those consistent with Judeo-Christian ethical teachings and rational thought, he combined them. Then Alfred went further.

He established one Common Law—one law for all—to encourage peace among different people. Its success depended on the hundreds of thousands of men and women who built on it over the next millennium. They tried to create a Common Law that was independent of kings and parliaments, and that evaluated the facts of individual cases rationally and fairly, respected precedent, defended freedom and responsibility and prevented injustice by seating community members as jurors. A Common Law is fundamental to communities of trust.

Alfred thought deeply and was a man of action. He hunted, translated books, fought invaders and built schools. He prayed daily, played music, and was an attentive husband and father.

When a friend, a partner or a beloved betrays us, we suddenly understand the meaning of trust.

Do not murder, do not commit adultery, do not steal, do not bear false witness, do not defraud....

—*Jesus*

The seed of virtue becomes a tree of life.

—*Proverbs*

GIFT 8

One Common Law that is Based on Judeo-Christian Ethics and is Clear, Fair and Merciful.

Alfred also understood that the law alone was not enough. He saw that men and women could not live, and his kingdom could not survive, without truth telling, promise-keeping and forgiveness. Only people who treat each other honestly can build community. Only they can create the next indispensable gift.

GIFT 9

Trust, Created by a Shared Culture of Honesty, Promise-keeping, Compassion and Forgiveness.

Without a widespread commitment to speaking the truth and acting with integrity, without people who refuse to steal or take bribes, a community cannot prosper no matter how many laws are on the books.

Alfred had one last gift to give. He opened schools to train students in riding and hunting, history, reading and writing English, logic and ethics.

But first, because so little was written in English, and he was one of the few people who knew Latin, Alfred sat down and translated books—Augustine's *Soliloquies*, Gregory's *Cura Pastoralis*, *The Consolation of Philosophy* by Boethius, the *Universal History* of Orosius. In the *History*, speaking directly to his English readers, he passionately condemned the Emperor Nero's lawlessness.

Alfred lived what he believed—

Your immortal soul has been given reason, memory and free will for a purpose.

He had found the door into the light.

GIFT 10

They shall build up the ancient ruins; they shall raise up the former devastations; they shall repair the ruined cities, the devastations of many generations.... For I the LORD love justice; I hate robbery and wrongdoing; I will faithfully give them their reward, and I will make an everlasting covenant with them.

—Isaiah

The Tor at Glastonbury was once an island surrounded by lake waters. It is said to be the place where Joseph of Arimathea came with the Holy Grail, St Patrick died, and King Arthur lived. As a boy, Dunstan studied with Irish monks on the island among the ruins. He became a harp-player, a monk, an ironsmith and a political reformer.

DUNSTAN WRESTLED in the 10th century with a problem we face today. The problem was at least as old as the Old Testament. In 1 Samuel, God had warned men that a king was a bad idea because he would try to enslave them. They stubbornly rejected this advice, and persuaded themselves that a king would protect them. There are valid reasons for wanting a leader, but a king or a president with unchecked power becomes toxic.

Working at the court of an English king, Dunstan protested injustice and immorality. Unfortunately, speaking the truth to despots could not please and did not change them. He was beaten within an inch of his life and thrown into a cesspool to drown. He escaped, but he was banished by two subsequent kings. He managed to rebuild desolate Glastonbury, but the problem of unjust leaders remained. In exile, Dunstan set himself the task of solving it.

The Anglo-Saxon *Witan* did their best to choose satisfactory kings, but they were not always successful. And good leaders did not always survive. Two kings friendly to Dunstan were assassinated. The challenge was keeping a leader just, responsive and alive.

In AD 960, sixteen-year-old Edgar was elected to the throne, and called Dunstan out of exile. Dunstan became Archbishop of Canterbury. On a wild island just outside London he built the monastery that would become Westminster Abbey. Meanwhile King Edgar did good work restoring schools, bridges and roads, but the leadership problem remained. How do you keep a king honest, and how do you ensure that his successors will be trustworthy? Kings (as well as presidents, prime

The idea of a covenant between leader and people will have momentous consequences for freedom and representative government—and for you personally.

ministers and religious leaders) are corrupted by unchecked authority, which corrodes their characters. How can their authority be limited and made accountable?

Like the ironsmith he was, Dunstan hammered out an answer in the hot forge of spiritual ideas and practical politics. His solution was a Covenant between people and leader and a Coronation Ceremony that made their mutual pledge sacred and spectacular.

In the Coronation Ceremony devised by Dunstan and used for a thousand years, the king swore a Coronation Oath before God to his people to defend their laws and customs; the people pledged to give the king their loyal support so long as he (or she) kept her promise. The Coronation ring was the symbol of their Covenant.

The Ceremony fused beauty and richness with the Judeo-Christian ideal of the leader as servant. This is made

A promise is 'rightly solemn, both because of the gravity of the responsibility to keep it and because of the danger of failing to keep it'.

—*Wendell Berry*

clear during the Communion service when the king or queen is stripped and, wearing only a white shirt, is anointed by a spiritual shepherd.

In 973, after thirty-year-old Edgar promised God and people that he would defend peace, equity and mercy and forbid extortion, Dunstan crowned him. Dunstan had set a standard for the next millennium. Today we know that a leader and people are bound together in a Covenant of freedom, justice and peace. The leader who breaks that Covenant deserves to be removed from office.

GIFT 10
A Covenant between People and Leader. The People Agree to Support a Leader as Long as He (or She) Defends Justice.

GIFT 11

Built by William the Conqueror in AD 1078, the Tower of London reeked of domination, but its architecture spoke silently of natural, spiritual and universal laws. Among these laws is the innate dignity of every individual.

ONE HUNDRED YEARS had passed since the first covenant promising justice had been made between king and people. In 1066, William the Conqueror swept into the islands. In 1100, his son, William II, the Red King, was on the throne.

The Conqueror had imposed *the fiction of tenure*—that all land belonged to him and all people were his tenants. But the people tenaciously defended their rights to their land and livelihood.

Breaking his covenant, the Red King attacked them. He robbed churches and seized common land—the forests—that had once belonged to all the people. Those who resisted him were blinded and castrated.

Uneasy lies the head that wears a crown.

—Shakespeare

William the Conqueror exploited his relationship with Edward the Confessor to legitimize seizing the English throne. The conquered English shrewdly connected Common Law with Edward the Confessor so the Conqueror and his Normans would respect it.

The New Forest, where the Red King was shot.

On August 2nd 1100, the Red King rode into the New Forest with his hunting party. Riding with him were his courtiers and his younger brother Henry. We know what happened next, but not why.

The Red King was shot dead with an arrow through his heart. Had Sir Walter Tyrrell missed a stag in the leafy forest, or had an unknown assailant hit his royal target? Was the king's death an accident or an assassination?

The body was placed in a cart. Henry and Robert de Beaumont galloped out of the New Forest to reach Winchester ahead of the dead king.

Henry wanted to get his hands on the royal treasury and the throne before his older brother, who had a better claim, arrived. He may have worried that another arrow was aimed at him. Robert de Beaumont, the best-educated man in the islands and one of the most powerful, looked with cool eyes at the dead king and thought about new possibilities.

A third man, whose unseen presence could be felt, was Anselm, Archbishop of Canterbury. He had opposed the Red King's oppressions. At the moment, he was out of the country.

Henry and Beaumont did not know whether Anselm would crown Henry on his return. But Beaumont was sure that the men who had endured the Red King's violence would want a change.

In August 1100, Henry was elected king and crowned at Westminster Abbey. He swore a Coronation Oath that would change the history of the West.

Beaumont told Henry that there was only one way he could be elected and crowned. He would have to swear a great oath to his knights and bishops. You might wonder if Henry understood the significance of his oath. He probably did. He had studied law and considered *an uneducated king to be a crowned ass.*

The oath established a new principle, and Henry, in a hurry, agreed to it. His oath, known as the Charter of Liberties, included a one-sentence pledge to restore the law of Edward the Confessor—that is, Common Law. From this promise flowed the gift that many people in the world still long to possess.

GIFT 11
Every Ruler Is Bound to Obey the Law. No One, Not Even the King, Is above the Law.

GIFT 12

Archbishop Anselm's first action when he returned to England in September of 1100 was to hear the plea of an Anglo-Saxon princess who had been shut away in a nunnery, and wanted to leave. *I wore the veil trembling as I wore it with indignation and grief,* she told him. *I used to snatch it from my head, fling it on the ground, and trample it under foot.*

FREEDOM ABSORBED ANSELM'S THOUGHTS—the freedom of the church, the freedom of a young girl and the freedom of the people of England. He

Anselm's rational proof for the existence of God arose out of conversations with his friends. He wrote dialogues on truth and free will.

had escaped his abusive father in Lombardy by crossing the Alps on foot when he was a teenager. After wandering across Europe, he found a home at Bec Abbey in Normandy. Respected and popular, he was elected abbot in his mid-forties. In 1093, he became Archbishop of Canterbury.

Today many people want government free of religion. Anselm wanted religion free of government. Unlike many others, he also wanted people to be free.

In 1100, British children were still being kidnapped into slavery. Contemporary chronicler William of Malmesbury wrote, *Young men and maidens whose beauty and youth might move the pity of the savage, were bound together with cords, and brought to market to be sold.*

Anselm loathed slavery. He ordered the princess in the nunnery to be freed. She married Henry I and became Queen Matilda, a loyal friend and supporter of Anselm and a patron of historian William of Malmesbury.

In 1102, Anselm called all the bishops and abbots to meet at the Council of Westminster. He was determined to end the abhorrent practice of slavery, which at the time was accepted throughout the world.

He told the assembled Christians that slavery was contrary to Christ's teaching. He urged them to condemn

We needed to stop asking about the meaning of life, and instead think of ourselves as those who were being questioned by life—daily and hourly.

–Viktor Frankl

it, and they did. The Council of Westminster declared, *Let no one hereafter presume to engage in that nefarious trade in which hitherto in England men were sold like brute animals.*

Unlike so many councils, this one had a positive effect. Slavery was outlawed. Slave traders knew that if they engaged in the trade the English Church would have them excommunicated, thereby rendering their property and lives forfeit.

At first this bequest was recognized only in England. Over the next nine centuries it will become one of our greatest gifts.

GIFT 12
Slavery is Repugnant and is Against the Law.

GIFTS 13, 14 & 15

Windsor Castle Tower. One hundred years passed. A new king—capricious, corrupt and cruel—sat on the throne of England. Men had forgotten their Inheritance.

The people of the islands lived in a country of forests, rivers, farms and small towns. Horses and dogs were their daily companions. Sailing the sea and riding spurred their love of liberty.

Knights learned to judge each other by answering the toughest question—Can I trust this man with my life?

WHO WOULD THEY BECOME? Would the people of England, Scotland and Wales remain cowed and ignorant of their Inheritance or would they become greater than they had ever been and rise up to defend their rights and liberties? Would the knights hear the call of justice, or become the weak creatures of selfishness? Would the archbishop defend the knights or would he creep to the side of King John? Would the Londoners and their mayor, Serlo the Mercer, try to appease the King or would they defy him?

Only one thing was certain—the choices they made would transform them.

In Old English the word knight meant servant. The knight was a servant to a lord, but which lord? How the knights answered that question in 1215 would change the course of history.

The life story of William Marshal reveals the dangers and opportunities that every knight faced. William Marshal was five or six years old when his father, who had quarreled with King Stephen, promised to keep his truce. He sent William as a hostage to the King, broke the truce and abandoned his son to die. Against all the odds, and with the help of his mother, William survived. He became a young squire who liked to eat, sleep and roughhouse.

Older knights taught the boy how to serve, how to ride and skill in arms. His horse taught him to be centered. His lord taught him to obey his commands, the Code of Chivalry and, for better or worse, how to be a man.

The Code required a man to be courageous and truthful, just and merciful, a Marian defender of women and children and a servant of God. Knights were supposed to treat a vanquished knight as their guest until his ransom was paid. If the captive knight had been wounded, they were to care for his injuries. The ideal of chivalry inspired some knights, but as William Marshal painfully learned when he was wounded and captured, not all of them.

What happened when the lord a knight was bound to obey was not chivalrous? The lord usually had the last word.

When he was in his early 20s, William Marshal was knighted. He spent the day and night before the ceremony fasting and praying. His sword lay on the altar as a sign that God's justice and mercy were to rule his actions. In the morning he bathed, dressed, confessed and went to Mass. He knelt before his lord and took a solemn vow to keep the laws of chivalry. His lord gave him the accolade—striking him on the shoulder with the flat side of his sword—and they celebrated his knighthood at a big dinner. William Marshal had just one problem.

❋

…belt your waist with truth; put on the breastplate of justice; shod your feet with the gospel of peace; lift the shield of faith…. And take up the helmet of salvation and the sword of the Spirit….

—Saint Paul

❋

On Flight 1549, which had crash landed in the Hudson River, passengers heard a single chivalrous cry of 'Women and children first'! Total strangers facing possible drowning stepped aside to let mothers and children pass.

Robert de Boron's verse romance about the Quest for the Holy Grail became popular a decade before the struggle for Magna Carta began. The knights would have heard it sung. Like many of us, knights were searching for greater meaning and purpose in life.

The Code of Chivalry is still alive in the Geneva Conventions, which call for the protection of civilians in time of war and for the humane treatment of captured combatants.

In the 15th century, Jeanne d'Arc showed that the knight's quest could belong to a woman as well as a man.

He had no money. He was forced to sell most of his clothes to buy a horse. To earn a living, he entered tournaments. He was brilliant at unseating opponents, and won large purses. But he really excelled in the mêlée of major tournaments when knights fought with sword and mace over several square miles. There success depended upon more than strength and skill—a knight had to be a player in a team game.

William became the greatest knight in Europe. Poignantly, he protected a father—Henry II—from attempted assassination by his sons. Defending Henry, Marshal unhorsed Richard the Lionheart. Later he helped the Knights Templar to protect pilgrims in the Holy Land. In his early forties, he married Isabel de Clare. He called her his *belle amie*.

Marshal became a CEO with a sword. He managed his working farms, kept lands and people safe, judged disputes and negotiated treaties. In exchange for his land, he owed taxes and military service to the king. Obliged to attend the king's court to protect his interests in England and Normandy, he travelled hundreds of miles on horseback every year.

The people of the islands cherished their land, which was also their livelihood.

Like many wives, Isabel ran the household and business when her husband was away. Other women had their own businesses. In the 13th century, *women traders and artisans in London formed a significant group within the city's workforce.*

Marshal and Isabel had five sons and five daughters whom they loved, as Marshal's biography, published by his eldest son, reveals. When John came to the throne in 1199, Marshal could not imagine that the King would threaten his children.

If you have ever suffered evil, you know that it can come like an illness—silently and without warning. People often prefer to ignore the small signs that appear. They're busy, and it's easier to ignore trouble or hope it will disappear. But like a serious illness, once evil has a foothold it incapacitates its victims.

So it was for the men and women who felt John's corruption slithering toward them. John used inducements or threats to achieve his ends and erupted into rages when thwarted. He erratically increased tax rates, eroding the people's ability to plan ahead and devastating commerce. He kept lands that his father Henry II had

...If you can dream—and not make dreams your master;

If you can think—and not make thoughts your aim;

If you can meet with triumph and disaster

And treat those two imposters just the same;

If you can bear to hear the truth you've spoken

Twisted by knaves to make a trap for fools,

Or watch the things you gave your life to broken,

And stoop and build 'em up with worn out tools;...

—Rudyard Kipling

seized, and cruelly punished those who took food or fuel from the forests he called his. He increased his grip on power by raising taxes and buying mercenaries. He perverted the course of justice, and he demanded that knights give him their sons and daughters as hostages. In short, John was the anti-knight.

John's actions outraged many knights. They included William d'Aubigny, who had tried to defend his people from John's sheriffs, William Marshal, Robert Fitzwalter, Roger Bigod, Robert de Vere, John de Lacy, William of Huntingfield, Geoffrey de Mandeville and Saer de Quincy. There were others.

Edward the Confessor holds the Coronation Ring that symbolizes the covenant of justice between king and people. King John willfully ignored the covenant.

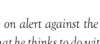

Be on alert against the king: what he thinks to do with me, he will do to each and every one of you, or even more, if he gets the upper hand.

—William Marshal

The Seal of Robert Fitzwalter. John confiscated Fitzwalter's inheritance and was accused of raping his daughter.

At the beginning of the 13th century, Marshal, who was in his fifties, was strong enough to scale a castle wall and flatten an opponent (though he sat down on the fellow's unconscious body to catch his breath). John wanted to recover the lands he had lost in France, but he had lost Marshal's respect. In 1205 Marshal refused point-blank to fight for him in Normandy.

Infuriated, John ordered the knights to challenge Marshal to armed combat. No one dared. Instead, they declined en masse to join the King's expedition across the Channel.

But King John had the power to lay siege to any knight's castle and destroy him. He forced Marshal to give his sons, William and Richard, as hostages. Marshal retreated to Ireland with Isabel and his remaining family. He was in exile for seven years.

The knights loathed John, but every knight was afraid to stick his head above the parapet. Each man feared that he and his family would be cut down.

John defeated the Scottish king, pillaged Ireland and invaded Wales. The Pope excommunicated him, but John viewed Pope and Church with indifference. Then, just when he seemed untouchable, the Welsh revolted, and the King of France made plans to invade.

William Marshal

Like many in this story, the contributions of the Welsh have been forgotten. After their rebellion in 1212, John hanged the twenty-eight young sons of Welsh princes who were his hostages. The Welsh would rise again.

On May 15th, 1213, in a cunning and unpopular manoeuvre, John knelt on the ground before the papal envoy, and surrendered England to the Pope. The Pope lifted the excommunication and forced the French king to back off. John made new plans to invade France.

A description of Christian contemplation can be found in The Cloud of Unknowing. *The 14th century English author, who has never been identified, wrote that contemplation is grounded in love.*

Again the knights baulked at going. One of them was the valiant and generous 'dwarf warrior', William de Mowbray, who stood with his friends. Enraged, John made plans to punish them.

One man stopped him. That man was Stephen Langton, the newly arrived Archbishop of Canterbury.

Contemplation gave men and women the certainty that God loved them and wanted them to establish justice on earth. Moses, Socrates, Julian of Norwich, and Saints Patrick, Brigid, Aidan, Anselm, Teresa and Francis were Christian contemplatives. So was Stephen Langton.

Stephen had been born in England in a moated farmhouse. At the University of Paris, he taught that Scripture called everyone to defend justice and help the poor. To John's disgust, Stephen was elected Archbishop of Canterbury and landed in England in 1213. He soon learned that the King wanted vengeance, and had ordered his mercenaries to punish the knights.

Stephen knew that a previous archbishop had been murdered for disagreeing with John's father, but he was the Lord's knight and he didn't hesitate. He warned the King that he faced excommunication and lawful rebellion by his subjects. Shaken, John called off his mercenaries.

Stephen was uninterested in praise or credit, which meant he could accomplish tremendous things. He also had a genuine interest in history. He knew that to forget the Inheritance is to lose it.

Stephen had waded through William of Malmesbury's somewhat disheveled account of English kings and archbishops. In one long sentence William had described Henry I *driving the flagitious from court and issuing an oath to uphold the law.* It was that oath of Henry's—the Charter of Liberties—that transfixed Stephen. He searched for the forgotten Charter, and found it.

On August 25th 1213, he gathered the knights at Westminster, and read the Charter of Liberties to them. They were dumbfounded to realize that Henry had established the great and liberating precedent—*even the king must obey the law.* The knights took a copy of the Charter with them when they left London.

But they were not ready to confront John. Over the next year, as they talked with friends and relatives, they began to rally around a cause greater than themselves.

The bridge at Wycoller, Lancashire, looks much as it did in the 13th century. Many Lancashire knights rode out to win justice from the King. They were buoyed by John's military defeat at the hands of the French people at Bouvines.

Anselm freed a young woman who became Queen Matilda and then William of Malmesbury's patron. (Gift 12). William's history contained the vital reference to the forgotten Charter of Liberties. One good deed can lead to another...

The bridge to the Abbey of Bury St Edmunds. On November 20th 1214, as leaves lay thick in the woods and on the roads, knights from around England rode to the abbey for a secret meeting.

In an environment where man and manhood are often subject to derision, it's important to celebrate good men who aren't afraid to recognize there's a power greater than their own. It's important to celebrate good men who know the right order of things....Their examples are living moral compasses in a confusing world.

−Kathryn Jean Lopez

Roger of Wendover, a Benedictine chronicler, describes the scene in the abbey—

> ...after they had discoursed together secretly for a time, there was placed before them the charter of King Henry the First, which they had received in the City of London from Stephen, Archbishop of Canterbury.

> ...They swore on the great altar that, if the king refused to grant these liberties and laws, they themselves would withdraw from their allegiance to him, and make war on him, till he should, by a charter under his own seal, confirm to them every thing they required.

They and many other people have endowed us with our next gift—

GIFT 13

To Hold the Liberties that are Ours by Right, and to Receive the Justice Due Us, We Have to be Willing to Risk Our Lives.

Temple Church, London, where the knights presented their demands to King John. The acoustics of the Templars' 12th century church will amplify a whisper.

In the New Year, 1215, the knights rode into London and to the Templars' church. Inside, they met King John, William Marshal and Stephen Langton. Marshal, who had won his sons' freedom, was serving as an intermediary between knights and King.

The knights declared that the King was transgressing against the laws and liberties of his people, and must make amends immediately. John said he'd get back to them. As soon as they left, he hired mercenaries from Europe to crush them.

Learning of the King's plans, the knights took the revolutionary step of renouncing their fealty, and gathering under arms. In May an army of knights led by Robert Fitzwalter mustered at Stamford and marched on London. They had at last become a team. They included Roger Bigod, William d'Aubigny and William Marshal's eldest son, William, Jr.

They called their army the Army of God and Holy Church. They were determined to succeed, but without the support of the people of England, Scotland and Wales, they would fail.

For centuries, the people of the islands had met in popular outdoor assemblies—*folkmotes*—where they evaluated evidence about property disputes and crime, and handled trade and the defence of their homes, towns and shires. The open-air gatherings often ended with a barbecue.

In the 11th century, in Bury St Edmunds, a farmer by the name of Ketel was accused of a crime he did not commit. He was denied a jury trial and executed. His grieved and angered neighbours protested fiercely, and established ever after the right to trial by jury in their community

The right to trial by jury came not from government but from the common sense of the people working together. Jury trials were established in many parts of the islands by the 12th century.

The folkmotes were one inspiration for Henry II's Assize of Clarendon, which formalized the status of juries and established grand juries in 1166.

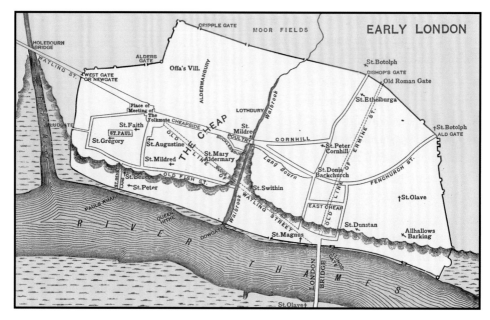

At the time of Magna Carta, London numbered 100,000 citizens. They had representative councils, appointed their own sheriffs and judges, set their own taxes, set up their own fire-companies and repeatedly resisted the high-handedness of sovereigns. Local control improved the quality of services. Trade was booming. You can see the site of the *folkmote* just above St Faith.

Magna Carta was won with the support of people from all over Britain It is strange to think that their contributions go unrecognized today.

A number of towns had charters of liberty, purchased with cash from kings and barons because townspeople believed it was crucial to their wellbeing to run their own communities. They were so committed to self-government they were prepared to pay for it. It was an innovative arrangement, and encouraged efficient and economical town management.

In London in May 1215, the citizens had recently elected a new mayor, Serlo the Mercer. He was a silk merchant and key to this story. John tried to win Serlo and Londoners to his side, but they were unmoved. Experience had taught them that John's word would tear like moth-eaten cloth.

When the banners of the Army of God fluttered into view, Serlo and the Londoners threw open the gates and welcomed them. Promises of help poured in from across England, Scotland and Wales.

Abandoned by one and all, John faced a nation in arms. William Marshal coolly pointed out the new realities to the King.

By then Stephen Langton knew that they would need more than a general admission from John that he would respect their liberty and laws. The knights, citizens of the towns, abbots and bishops and free men of the shires and Wales would have to specify every freedom and act of justice they wanted.

Motivated by common sense, Common Law, the teachings of Christ and their own self-interest, they drafted more than sixty clauses, including some of the most life-affirming protections of freedom and justice ever seen. When they were done, they had filled a large page of vellum that would become known ever after as Magna Carta, the Great Charter of Liberty.

In June, when the verges were green with grass and white with flowers, William Marshal and the knights and Stephen Langton and the abbots, bishops and representatives of the towns rode to Runnymede, a meadow beside the River Thames. It lay not far from the King's castle at Windsor. They carried Magna Carta with them. The knights were armed.

On June 15th 1215, in their presence and under the open sky, John agreed to Magna Carta.

The language used in Magna Carta was Latin. The ink was made of crushed oak apples, sulphate of iron, gum and water.

In 1994, the Prime Minister of India left a plaque at Runnymede that reads: 'As a tribute to historic Magna Carta, a source of inspiration throughout the world, and as an affirmation of the values of Freedom, Democracy and the Rule of Law which the People of India cherish and have enshrined in their Constitution'.

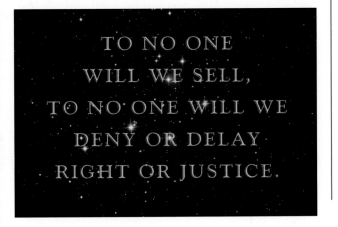

TO NO ONE
WILL WE SELL,
TO NO ONE WILL WE
DENY OR DELAY
RIGHT OR JUSTICE.

Copies were made and sent out under the King's seal to every cathedral and town. Back in Windsor Castle, John threw himself on the floor and screamed with fury.

GIFT 14

RIGHTS AND LIBERTIES ENSHRINED IN MAGNA CARTA

- The right to trial by jury.

- The right to habeas corpus ('you have the body'). —We cannot be arrested and kept in prison indefinitely without being charged and tried under the law of the land.

- The right to own property, which cannot be taken from us without due payment or process of law.

- The right not to be fined so heavily as to have our livelihood destroyed.

- The right to reasonable taxation levied only with the general consent of the kingdom.

- The right of the Church to be free from government control.

- The right of London and other cities, towns, and ports to have all their liberties and customary freedoms.

- The right to travel freely in and out of the country except during war.

- These rights to be observed not only by the king but by all men.

The Welsh had their lands and liberties restored by Magna Carta. Foreign mercenaries were expelled, and hostages were returned to their families. The establishment of an advisory council, which could check the King and provide redress, planted the seed of representative government.

The people gathered in the meadow did not know that over the next 800 years Magna Carta would become a highway to freedom. Only a few of them guessed that within months they would be fighting for the Great Charter, and for their lives.

The King spent a few surly weeks considering his options then asked the Pope to annul Magna Carta. The Pope declared Magna Carta invalid, and ordered Stephen to excommunicate the rebels, thereby rendering their lives and possessions forfeit.

A triumphant John threw off his mask and prepared to wreak revenge. But once again he had underestimated Stephen Langton.

Defying the Pope, Stephen refused to excommunicate the knights and destroy the rebellion. Defying the King, he held Rochester Castle and refused to surrender it to him. The castle was crucial to protecting London from the King's army.

The Pope ordered Stephen to appear before him in Rome. Langton turned Rochester Castle over to William d'Aubigny, a supporter of Magna Carta. John relentlessly attacked with siege engines, but d'Aubigny held the castle, giving the rebels time to regroup, until he was starved into surrender. John moved to attack the remaining knights with fire and sword.

Roger Bigod led the resistance in the north. Wales rose in rebellion. William Marshal held Pembroke Castle, and refused to help the King. The first knight to be named in Magna Carta, Marshal pondered his next move.

Magna Carta was the first political document in history to assert the human rights of individuals. Carried around the world, Magna Carta helped to establish freedom and just law in America, Canada, India, Australia and New Zealand. Out of the rule of just law comes prosperity.

IN PRAISE OF OLDER MEN

William d'Aubigny helped to establish Magna Carta and defended the Great Charter against John's siege engines. He was 64 in 1215.

Robert Fitzwalter, who led the Army of God, was in his 60s.

Stephen, Archbishop of Canterbury, was 65 in 1215. In 1225, when he was 75, Stephen had Magna Carta reissued for a second time by Henry III.

William Marshal was 69 in 1215 and 71 when he had Magna Carta reissued, and fought the French.

Roger Bigod, the linchpin of northern resistance to John, was 72.

Without these older men, Magna Carta would never have been and could never have survived its first years of existence.

Rochester Castle

The rebel knights refused to submit. In desperation they asked the French Dauphin and his knights for help.

In October 1216, John lost part of his baggage train and his jewels while crossing the Wash, and died. William Marshal went into action to handle three emergencies.

One issue still smoldered— the forest.

He had John's young son crowned Henry III. He reissued Magna Carta and affirmed that the new King would honour it. And he rode into battle with William, Jr., and d'Aubigny to expel the French, who wanted to seize England and were loath to leave.

For centuries, the people will depend on and defend the rights and liberties enshrined in Magna Carta.

In the forest the islanders felt free, far from the demands of manor or plough, baron, church or king. Inhaling the pure, sweet air, they moved with every sense wide open and awake. Wolves and boar lurked in the thickets. Spotted fawns lay hidden in the long grass, and in the clearings the great red stag strode through the dawn mist.

The forest was sanctuary and provider. Here was venison—good meat—and fuel for the fire and wood to build a house—until kings declared the forest was theirs and shut the people out.

Indeed, in their effrontery and greed, kings used the word forest to mean far more than the greenwood. They called *towns, villages and farms*—and the entire counties of Cornwall and Devon—their forest.

If your home was in the king's 'forest', you could be fined for clearing your land and planting vegetables. If you killed a deer for dinner, you could be blinded. Whole communities were prosecuted if the offender was not found. The *iniquities of the royal forest system united rich and poor alike in opposition to the Crown.*

At Runnymede, the reformers demanded that all the 'forests' taken by Richard I and Henry II be given back and the *evil customs* of forest justice be ended, but John returned only a small portion of the land that had been seized. When he died, the council governing on behalf of his son acted swiftly.

In 1217 the council issued the Charter of the Forest, which returned to the people all the forestland taken by Henry II, Richard I and John. This act of justice reestablished the ancient right of shared common resources—a vital principle and gift that will develop into our shared right to bridleways and footpaths, public roads, parks and airwaves.

GIFT 15

The People's Right to Share Certain Common Lands and Resources.

GIFT 16

The bachelor knights made their last stand at Kenilworth Castle. Their courage will give life to a new creation.

If a nation values anything more than freedom, it will lose its freedom; and the irony of it is that if it is comfort or money that it values more, it will lose that too.

—W. Somerset Maugham

IF ONLY PROGRESS proceeded in a straight line. But as our own lives reveal, we sometimes regress before moving forward. So in the islands, a great advance had been made with Magna Carta. But four decades later, under John's son Henry III, the islanders were facing some of the same evils that had inspired their earlier revolt.

The bachelor knights of England were young and energetic. Their blood boiled at the corruption and violence of Henry III's sheriffs and the profiteering of Crown bureaucrats.

At the court of Henry III, the administration passed into the hands of men who were contemptuous of Common Law and honest government.

The knights were not alone in wanting the shackles of misgovernment removed. Village constables, university students, farmers, fishermen, blacksmiths, carpenters, Londoners and merchants, the great earls of England, bishops and abbots were all united in opposing injustice, high taxes and arrogant, self-dealing government— many of the same things people are opposing today. Two men were their leaders. Both carried the surname Montfort, but they were not related.

Simon de Montfort had arrived in England to recover the inheritance left him by his grandmother. Bold, cultured and arrogant, a superb soldier, Montfort fell in love with Henry III's sister, Eleanor. After they eloped, Simon personally experienced the King's humiliating and capricious injustice.

Montfort respected Robert Grosseteste, the scientist-bishop, though the bishop had plainly rebuked him when he treated a merchant unfairly. Grosseteste sent Montfort an essay on tyranny. For the first time Montfort saw unchecked power as an immoral cause of misery for himself personally and for the community at large. He began to consider what he could do about it.

Coat of Arms of the town of Oxford. Townspeople and students supported the reforms.

John of Salisbury's Policraticus (AD 1159) famously described the difference between a prince and a tyrant—a prince upholds just law and equity.

The word 'parliament' comes from the French word for talk.

The reforms had a debilitating weakness— there was no way to enforce them.

Peter de Montfort was a good horseman, an excellent swordsman, and a cool and skilled mediator in the hectic campaigns of the 13th century. He held the castle of Beaudesert, not far from Simon de Montfort's Kenilworth Castle. Peter was close to his eldest son, Piers, who was one of the young bachelor knights calling for reform. Fathers and sons, friends and neighbors met together, talking about what they could do to restore justice to government.

In 1258, Simon, Peter, Piers and a host of knights and bachelor knights met in Oxford to protest against the King's tyranny. They swore a sacred oath and embarked on a campaign *imbued with the ideal of justice for all.*

Together they compelled the King to agree to the revolutionary Provisions of Oxford. The Provisions called for honest sheriffs, restricted to one-year terms, and forbade using church funds for war. They established a council that would meet three times a year as a "parliament" to approve or reject taxes, discuss affairs of the realm and advise the king. In 1259 they pushed through the Provisions of Westminster to help tenants with grievances against their lords.

Peter and Simon de Montfort helped to begin the revolution, and they drew up the plans for reform. People in the shires and towns supported the Provisions, but some of the big barons, disliking the reforms designed to curb their power, began to sidle away.

Initial success turned to dust. Henry III *gnawed and tunnelled like a rat*, undermining the Provisions with bribes, threats, delays and administrative sleight of hand. His son, Prince Edward, heir to the throne, refused to give his support, and the barons ignored the tenant reforms they had pledged to enact.

In 1264, the King repudiated the Provisions and fielded an army to punish the reformers. Peter de Montfort and Piers set out to support the reforms, and were captured in Northampton after the city was betrayed. The army

Lewes Castle. The prince's cavalry swept out from the castle gate and thundered toward the Londoners.

of Henry III and Prince Edward encamped at Lewes. Riding with a broken leg, Simon de Montfort led the reformers. Joined by Londoners, they marched by night to take the army of the King and prince by surprise. Montfort offered peace if the King would obey the Provisions. Henry III scornfully refused. His army outnumbered the reformers by two to one.

On May 14th, Montfort took the centre of the battle line, opposite the King. The Londoners were on his left. The charge of the prince's cavalry put the Londoners to flight. The furious prince and his men pursued them. It is said that they killed 3,000. The prince's actions were cruel and unwise. Returning hours later, he found the battle lost. The reformers had defeated the royal army, and captured the King. Edward became a prisoner. Peter and Piers were released from prison.

England breathes in the hope of liberty…Let the community of the realm advise, and let it be known what they think.

—A poet writing after the battle of Lewes

Magna Carta established standardized weights and measures, so when you bought a pound of corn or a pint of beer you weren't cheated. This helped families, improved trade and is the kind of useful work we look for from a parliament.

Governments that are answerable to their own people and accountable to a rule of law tend to respect the rights of their neighbors, honor their treaty commitments, and abide by the international rules of the road... Regimes that prey on their own citizens are likely to prey on their neighbors...

—Bret Stephens

The reformers invited the shires and towns to elect representatives and send them to a national parliament. On January 20th 1265, representatives from all over England gathered in Westminster and met as an elected parliament. It was a momentous step toward a government that represents all the people.

This historic act has been called a pragmatic gesture to generate support. It may well have been, but there's no reason why idealism shouldn't be practical. The gifts often unite the practical and ideal.

In its first act, Parliament affirmed the reforms, and the government prepared to enforce them. It looked like a triumph. Then Prince Edward escaped. Barons who feared that Simon de Montfort was growing too powerful deserted the cause and joined the prince.

As their forces dwindled through the summer of 1265, Simon, Peter, Piers and the bachelor knights remained loyal to the cause of reform. In August, they camped in the Vale of Evesham. They hoped to join forces with Simon's son, who was bringing reinforcements, and march to London, where support for the cause remained strong. With them was the captive King, whom they treated with courtesy.

On the morning of August 4th, they saw banners approaching. Too late they realized that Prince Edward had ambushed Simon de Montfort's son and captured his flags. The army of the prince surrounded the reformers.

On that summer morning, the Montforts understood that Edward wanted them dead. But unlike those who hide behind children and women and fire from schools and houses of worship, the Montforts refused to use the captive King as a pawn or to exploit Evesham Abbey for military purposes.

Simon de Montfort gathered the young bachelor knights around him, and urged them to surrender and support the reforms at a future time and place. Piers and the bachelors refused to abandon him or the cause.

The sky darkened under an approaching storm. Simon de Montfort looked at the army opposing them, and said—

They have our bodies; God has our souls.

Unless a grain of wheat falls into the earth and dies, it remains alone, but if it dies, it bears much fruit.

—Jesus

The Vale of Evesham, where the Montforts and the bachelor knights fought to defend the reforms.

Fathers and sons spurred their horses into battle, and charged uphill. They fought valiantly even as their circle grew smaller. Simon's eldest son was killed. Piers was wounded. Peter was killed. Fighting on almost alone, Simon was killed and his body was hacked into pieces.

The surviving bachelor knights and reformers regrouped and held Kenilworth Castle, the Isle of Ely, the Cinque Ports and the forests of Hampshire for two years. During that time the forces of the King took their homes and lands. They became *The Dispossessed*. Piers lost everything except his principles.

The resistance of The Dispossessed and the islanders' stubborn support for the reforms created an unforeseen change. Out of their sacrifice came new life.

Houses of Parliament, London. Over the course of a decade, the ideas for which the knights and the people of England had died took root. The prince, who was now King Edward I, agreed to the reforms. In 1275, the Statute of Westminster affirmed Parliament and the principle of honest elections.

A portrait of Simon de Montfort hangs in the US House of Representatives as a tribute to the man who helped to lay the foundations of representative government.

The Dispossessed eventually regained the land they had lost by paying heavy fines. Piers donated a substantial part of his recovered inheritance to help a friend build Merton College, Oxford.

The gift they helped to create was aimed primarily at holding a ruler accountable. Over the years, it would grow.

GIFT 16

Parliamentary Government Representing the People.

In the future, the struggle to confirm the representative rights and powers of the people and to establish a constitution setting forth those rights will blaze across the kingdoms and colonies of Britain.

GIFT 17

In the 13th century, scientists in the islands were studying the tides, eclipses, comets, the origins of sounds and the movements of planets. Five insights will help them and future scientists generate scientific discoveries.

BORN IN THE LATE 12TH CENTURY to a poor family, Robert Grosseteste had brains, curiosity and energy, but no money to go to school. Adam of Wigford—one of generations of men and women who helped poor children in the islands—paid his way. Grosseteste, a big six-footer, left school fascinated by the universe.

When he was in his 20s, he went to Hereford Cathedral, the most active centre of scientific studies in England. There, scientists were inspired by ideas crucial to Christianity and scientific exploration.

First, they grasped the indispensable role of truth—a lesson gleaned from Scripture and life. Their research confirmed truth's importance to science. Second, they realized that the human mind could think rationally. They assumed that God had given them reason, and they came to a natural conclusion—they were meant to understand God's world rationally.

Socrates questioned most opinions, but never doubted the existence of truth, goodness, beauty and God: 'Virtue does not come from money, but from virtue comes money and every good thing to the person and to the community.' His knowledge was based on understanding 'I do not think I know what I do not know'.

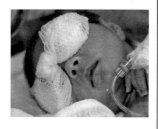

Some people have claimed that the truth is whatever anyone wants to believe it is. But few think the truth is a matter of opinion when a surgeon is operating on their child or a pilot is flying their plane.

By the 13th century, Englishmen had obtained Arabic astronomical data. They were making celestial and computational studies of their own and trying to answer an essential question—how do we prove the truth of these observations and calculations?

In his book *Posterior Analytics*, Aristotle grounded scientific knowledge in *elenchus*, the Socratic method, and credited Socrates with the development of inductive reasoning and universal definitions. Reading Aristotle on Socrates, Grosseteste had a Eureka! moment.

This came when he realized that the Socratic method could be used to test the validity of observations, calculations, theories and conclusions.

Searching for the physical laws and mathematical structures that were invisible to him, but which he believed governed the cosmos, Grosseteste taught that—

1. *From specific observations you may be able to infer a theory or to demonstrate that a theory is false.*

2. *If your theory holds water, you should be able to predict certain facts and outcomes.*

3. *You must constantly test your conclusions.*

These ideas inspired Roger Bacon, who was called *Doctor Mirabilis*. Bacon studied mathematics, optics, the natural sciences and physics. He wrote the formula for gunpowder in code to keep it secret. He predicted the inventions of the airplane, submarine and robot.

Bacon added two guidelines to the three described by Grosseteste. All five will be key to the development of science and the inventions we depend on today.

4. *Mathematics is necessary to science.*

5. *Use controlled experiments to test your hypothesis.*

Some people—including most professional politicians—never try to test their ideas. Scientists do test theories and as a result have helped to double our life expectancy and improve the quality of our lives.

Good scientists try to protect their ideas from political, religious or financial pressures. The traps set for scientists were systematically described in the 20th century—and they are snares for us as well.

One trap is *availability cascade*—an idea becomes irresistible because the authorities and the media keep repeating it. A secret snare is *availability bias*—we judge an idea's truth by how easily it comes to mind.

The *information cascade* occurs when the opinions of the crowd overwhelm independent thought. The fourth trap, particularly detested by Roger Bacon, is *reputation cascade*—a person is moved to change his opinion to improve his reputation, or save his bacon.

If I have seen further it is by standing on the shoulders of giants.

—Isaac Newton

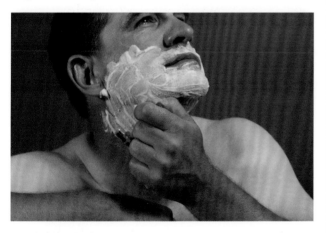

A philosopher and a Franciscan friar who worked in the 14th century, William of Ockham made a contribution to scientific thought known as *Ockham's Razor*. His idea was that *the simplest explanation with the least assumptions is probably the right one*. Ockham's Razor has remained sharp all these years.

Keeping in mind these scientific principles, and building and expanding on them, the people of the islands were on their way to creating an extraordinary number of modern inventions. Even the Black Death, which killed one in every three persons in the 14th century,

Get the facts, or the facts will get you. And when you get them, get them right, or they will get you wrong.

—Dr. Thomas Fuller

William of Ockham believed that God is not arbitrary, and the laws of nature are reliable.

Some people have a tendency to 'seek information that confirms what they already believe' rather than 'consider evidence that would challenge those beliefs'. The tendency is called confirmation bias. Scientists are scientists because they can overcome this bias.

could not stop them, though it did slow them down. But there was another reason for their inventiveness—*freedom.*

Scientists are like lovers—they pursue the objects of their desire. They can't be told what to desire—they must be free to choose. The fellow who worked out the structure of the atom did not have a burning desire to build a flush toilet. The woman who worked out the structure of penicillin so it could be mass-produced had no interest in inventing the knitting machine.

Freedom is essential to scientific progress. As freedom increased, so did scientific development. But there was another reason for their success—*they respected work.*

Ernest Shackleton made an 800-mile journey in an open boat through stormy seas to save his men on Elephant Island (above). Explorers use the scientific method and achievements to make discoveries and return home alive.

Successful societies treasure the work of hands and brains. They protect freedom and they nurture teachers and students.

Practical inventions, medical advances, cosmic discoveries and prosperity depend on this gift—

> Biotechnology could be a great equalizer, spreading wealth over the world wherever there is land and air and water and sunlight.
>
> — *Freeman Dyson*

GIFT 17

The Truth is Something We Can Rely On. Scientific Truth Can Be Verified.

It's a practical concept that can help to guide us—*if something is true it is consistent with the facts.*

GIFT 18

Sometime in the 12th century, decades before Magna Carta, students started Oxford University so they could have a liberal education.

Built in the 18th century to house a science library at Oxford, the Radcliffe Camera was paid for by physician John Radcliffe.

THE WORD *liberal* shares the same root as the word liberty. Christians believed that liberal meant free to enquire and investigate and that a liberal education would free a student from the chaos of irrationality. Two kings, 47 Nobel Prize winners (and counting), 25 British and Commonwealth prime ministers, several great poets, and 12 saints have studied or taught at Oxford since it was founded more than 800 years ago.

Walter de Merton's vision of a self-governing community of scholars living together in a college that consisted of four halls built around a quadrangle became a reality in the 13th century and a model for future universities.

A Cambridge quad. In 1209, after numerous brawls with Oxford townspeople, a group of students decamped and founded Cambridge University.

Today, Cambridge University numbers over 100 departments, colleges, and research institutes and more Nobel Prize winners than any other institution in the world. Many of the world's major scientific discoveries, including splitting the atom and DNA, were made at the university. Can all this be attributed to a fondness for reason and freedom, honesty and hard work?

As you've guessed, we need something else.

Just law and communities of trust are also crucial to science—if only because people who are constantly defending themselves from violence and injustice do not have much time for scientific discovery. In Britain hundreds of science societies, beginning with the Royal Society, shared information and conducted essential peer review. Competition, teamwork and the thrill of discovery inspired innovation and invention.

Great Hall at St. Bartholomew's Hospital, London. The plaques on the walls list the hospital's many benefactors.

Since 1609 the charity known as Sackville College has provided housing for older folk. Step through the door and you find their apartments in four buildings grouped around a peaceful quad.

Scientific innovation stimulated entrepreneurship, and entrepreneurs created prosperity. As they did, donors built and endowed schools, colleges, hospitals and libraries. This is synergy at its best—rational, inspiring, life-enhancing.

Buildings were built to endure, to shelter generations of men and women, to be beautiful and to welcome us. They are part of our Inheritance.

GIFT 18

Colleges and Universities, Scientific Societies, Art Academies, Research Hospitals and Beautiful, Useful and Durable Buildings.

GIFTS 19 & 20

John and Elizabeth Lilburne stood together in defying a government that tried to crush freedom of conscience. Persecution taught them that freedom of religion and the freedoms of speech, assembly and association are linked. Religious intolerance threatens all the gifts.

JOHN LILBURNE was in his teens when he left Thickley Punchardon in County Durham to become an apprentice in London. A few years later, in 1637, when he was in his twenties, he watched three friends have their ears cropped—sliced right off their heads—in a public spectacle. They were religious dissenters who refused to worship as the government ordered.

For several centuries, so-called Christians had martyred Christians who held beliefs not sanctioned by the government. The Greek word *martyr*, which means witness-bearer, entered English to describe the men and women who bore witness to freedom of conscience even if it meant dying in sheets of flame.

I was an honest poor man's daughter, never brought up in the university as you have been, but I have driven the plough before my father many a time, I thank God. Yet notwithstanding, in the defence of God's truth and in the cause of my master Christ, I will set my foot against the foot of any of you.

—Alice Driver to her persecutors before she was burned at the stake

...the bright red thread of human history is...liberty on trial.

—Michael Novak

Witnessing the mutilation of his friends, Lilburne was sick with fear—but not for long. He believed he had a God-given right to think, speak and worship freely. He began printing and distributing books banned by the government.

Informers employed by the state betrayed him. Lilburne was brought before the Star Chamber, a secretive arm of government where political and religious dissenters were condemned without appeal. There was no jury and the same people served as interrogators and judges, so the government could wring out the result it wanted. Victims, especially those who did not confess, received enormous fines and terrible punishments.

In the Star Chamber, John Lilburne's interrogators demanded that he confess to distributing banned literature. Lilburne refused to accuse himself. He told them he had a right to be silent under Common Law. His judges added insufferable disobedience and contempt to their accusations and had him tied to the back of a cart and flogged 200 times while being dragged across London from Fleet prison to the New Palace Yard where he was pilloried.

At the risk of his life, William Tyndale translated the Scriptures into English so that everyone—even boys and girls working in the fields—could understand what Scripture said and decide its meaning for themselves. Tyndale was in his early forties when, in 1536, he was betrayed, tied to a stake outside Brussels, strangled, and burned.

With his head and arms clamped in the pillory, Lilburne told the crowd that the Star Chamber was illegal. The government threw him back into prison, and had him shackled.

Unjust imprisonment can toughen a person. Lilburne refused to admit any guilt. His Christian faith sustained him. He continued to write. Supporters brought him food and smuggled out his political pamphlets. One of his visitors was Elizabeth Dewell. She had courage, and she shared his passion for liberty.

Who am I if I cannot freely say what I think?

Shakespeare, who died in 1616 shortly after Lilburne was born, had created heroines who were wise, witty and true, tender, just and brave. Shakespeare's women married for love, a rarity in the world then. Elizabeth Dewell and John Lilburne fell in love.

Public outrage about Lilburne's treatment grew. Parliament freed him in 1640, and abolished the Star Chamber in 1641. Not long after, John and Elizabeth married. Their campaign had just begun.

Lilburne's gift shields us from an overweening state's despotic interrogations and torture.

GIFT 19
We Have the Right to be Silent in the Face of Interrogation. We Have the Right to Refuse to Condemn Ourselves in a Court of Law.

Charles I had the unpleasant habit of breaking his promises.

For centuries new taxes had to be approved by Parliament—a right established in Magna Carta—but Charles I didn't want to call Parliament into session in case his policies were challenged. Instead he demanded loans from individuals. In 1627, MP John Hampden and his uncle refused to give the King his forced loans. Hampden was confined for a year. His uncle died in prison.

In 1634, Charles tried to turn the Crown's right to commandeer ships for defence into a permanent revenue stream. Lacking Parliament's approval, this was unconstitutional taxation.

Once again John Hampden defended Parliament and the Constitution and refused to pay. Once again he was taken to court. The proceedings were mobbed. The judges narrowly ruled against him. Hampden, pictured above, became a national hero.

Parliament's 1628 Petition of Right reaffirmed the principle that a person cannot be arrested because he or she disagrees with the government. Charles I ignored the principle and the Petition.

Aberdeen lighthouse

The principle of no taxation without representation will stand like a lighthouse in stormy political seas for future generations on both sides of the Atlantic.

Memorials to Robert the Bruce and William Wallace, who fought for Scottish independence from English rule, stand in Stirling.

In 1320, in the Declaration of Arbroath, the Scots had asserted—

> *It is in truth not for glory, nor riches, nor honours that we are fighting, but for freedom—for that alone, which no honest man gives up but with life itself.*

Beginning in 1637, the Scots began a struggle for freedom of conscience against Charles I. Charles demanded that the Scots worship as he directed. The Scots resisted then invaded England. The English people refused to fight them.

Conflict intensified between King and Parliament. Flouting long-established customs of freedom and covenant, Charles asserted his erroneous belief that he had a divine right to rule and was consequently not accountable to his subjects. In 1642 the islands erupted in Civil War, with Parliamentarians battling the King and his supporters.

Both John Lilburne and John Hampden fought for Parliament with distinction. Hampden died. Lilburne was captured and sent to Royalist headquarters to be executed for treason.

Elizabeth was pregnant, but she managed to obtain a memo from Parliament, and personally carried it to Royalist headquarters. Its simple message—*we will treat your prisoners exactly as you treat ours*—won Lilburne's release.

It is a curious and depressing aspect of history that those who have been oppressed sometimes become oppressors. Parliament had struggled to assert its freedoms, but even before it defeated and executed Charles I, it had become increasingly authoritarian and religiously dogmatic. In 1645, when John Lilburne insisted on freedom of speech and freedom of religion, Parliament had him thrown into Newgate.

Elizabeth joined him. She gave birth to their daughter in prison. Despite incarceration, Lilburne continued to write about the *freeborn rights* that belonged to every man and woman. After her release, Elizabeth circulated John's *Agreement of the People*. A third of all Londoners showed their support by signing it.

Lilburne asserted that he could only be charged under laws already on the books and that he had a right to a jury trial with all its safeguards. He declared—

> I have a right to all the privileges that do belong
> to a free man . . . and the ground and foundation
> of my freedom I build upon the Great Charter
> of England.

Thousands shared Lilburne's ideas. They called themselves Agitators. (Opponents called them Levellers.) The Agitators wanted the right to vote, political and social equality and religious tolerance.

Emerging as one of their leaders, Lilburne was ahead of his time in calling for representative government with the people holding 'unalienable' rights, including freedom of speech, religion, assembly and trade.

The rights of man come not from the generosity of the state but from the hand of God.

—US President John F. Kennedy

Those in power feared these ideas and the people who held them. Parliament's grandees and Oliver Cromwell, the head of the Army, crushed the Agitators and the soldiers who supported them. They were not able to silence Lilburne.

Elizabeth was ill, and had just lost two children to smallpox. She felt they had done enough. But John continued to protest against the military dictatorship. In 1649, Parliament charged him with treason.

Lilburne successfully persuaded his jury that they were judges of law as well as fact. If they believed a law to be unjust, they could and should refuse to convict. In a packed court, the jury pronounced John Lilburne innocent. Londoners celebrated with bonfires.

But those who were in power hated his ideas and found new ways to attack him. Lilburne spent the next decade in prison and exile and died at the age of 42.

Lilburne's ideas did not die. The torch he had lit and carried with the help of his wife Elizabeth was passed to another.

William Penn was not the stodgy fellow you may have met in history books. He was athletic, daring and brave. A few decades after Lilburne's death, he defied an unjust law and changed history.

In the 1660s, Friends, also known as Quakers, were being attacked and imprisoned for their religious views. Penn, although he was only twenty-two, defended them. This made him a pariah.

Penn began working with George Fox and his wife Margaret Fell. Both of them had been incarcerated for bearing witness to freedom of religion. Together they established the principles that alarmed sedate society—

> No church has authority over the individual. All people are equal under God, and every person can experience a relationship with God. Friends ought to reject titles and vanities. Government ought to allow freedom of religion.

In response, the government viciously persecuted the Friends. Penn was jailed, and placed in solitary confinement for eight months. He was told to recant. He refused.

Released in 1670, at the age of 26, Penn deliberately gathered a crowd in a public street in London to test the new law against freedom of assembly.

He was arrested. In court, Penn mounted a brilliant defence against the charge of disturbing the peace and claimed that he could not be found guilty of a law that was unjust and illegal. The court had him gagged.

As the jury left the courtroom to decide whether he was guilty, Penn managed to call out, *Ye are Englishmen . . . give not away your right!*

His jurors doggedly answered, *Nor will we ever!*

On September 5th 1670, the jurors delivered a verdict of innocent because they believed that the law against assembly was unjust.

Izaak Walton skillfully cast a message of religious tolerance into his classic on fishing, The Compleat Angler.

12

Given 12 inches to the foot, 12 months to the year, and 12 disciples of Christ, 12 seemed like the right number for a jury—enough jurors to take a hard look at the evidence without being cowed by prosecutors or seduced by the defence.

Jurors have a right to determine both the law as well as the fact in controversy.

*— John Jay
First Chief Justice of the
US Supreme Court*

The enraged judge sent them back to deliberate until they reached a verdict of guilty. The jurors refused. The judge had them jailed with Penn in urine-soaked and rat-infested Newgate Prison.

Eight of the jurors broke. Four held out for nine weeks. Edward Bushell, the jury foreman, managed to have a writ of habeas corpus taken to the Lord Chief Justice of the High Court, Sir John Vaughn.

To the government's consternation, the High Court ruled that the jury had a right to return a verdict of not guilty, and, further, that the jury did not have to explain its verdict.

Penn and the jurors had established forever the legal doctrine that it is the jury's right and responsibility to decide *whether the law under which a person has been charged is just.* In fulfilling this mission, jurors become the conscience of the community and a line of defence against oppression.

Thomas Jefferson later wrote, *I consider trial by jury as the only anchor yet imagined by man by which a government can be held to the principles of its constitution.*

GIFT 20
Juries Have the Power and Duty to Refuse to Convict When They Believe that the Law Is Unjust.

In winning his case, William Penn established that freedom of speech, freedom of religion, freedom of assembly and the freedom of juries are connected—as closely as your heart and lungs and the blood circulating through your body. In the following decade, he began to explore a new and visionary idea.

GIFT 21

Pennsylvania. Many people who wanted 'soul liberty' and economic opportunity looked toward the New World.

DEFYING THE DANGERS of ocean and wilderness, 17th century men, women and children sailed west with their dogs for America. They intended to build communities where they could worship freely and make a new start. They were full of hope. Reality was a bit different, especially for those who were indentured.

In New York, the authorities prohibited freedom of religion despite protests. In Massachusetts, some settlers became intolerant of religious beliefs different from their own. Still others made the colony of Rhode Island a safe place for people of all religions, only to see the colony pulled apart by factions. They rather urgently needed a new way of doing things.

Life is short,
and we do not have much
time to gladden the hearts of
those who journey with us.
Be swift to love!
Make haste to be kind.

—Henri-Frédéric Amiel

Penn State elms. Penn had a green rule—protect and plant trees.

Pennsylvania helped to prepare the way for a national constitution that respected and protected the 'unalienable' rights of individuals.

William Penn managed to persuade luxury-loving Charles II that a colony that guaranteed religious tolerance would prosper. The idea appealed to the King because he hoped to profit from it and he wanted to ship the Friends overseas.

Charles owed Penn money. Since he preferred to pay with a grant to land he arguably did not own, he gave Penn 45,000 square miles in America.

In 1682, Penn left Britain to establish the colony of Pennsylvania. (The King insisted on the name.) Penn had the King's grant, but the land belonged to Native Americans. He won their trust by being brave enough to negotiate without carrying a weapon and (always helpful) by paying them for their land. They made their treaty under the shade of an elm.

Penn published a unique form of real estate promotion—the Pennsylvania constitution, which he wrote. The constitution established freedom of religion and representative government, fair taxes, free elections, a limit to executive power, the protection of free enterprise and trial by jury. It proved irresistible, and contained the innovation of being amendable. Pennsylvania and Pennsylvanians thrived.

Penn and many unsung individuals contributed to a remarkable new development. They helped to create a gift of peace and healing—

GIFT 21

Freedom of Religion and Religious Tolerance. Every Individual Has the Right to Worship as He or She Chooses — Or Not to Worship At All.

There is a caveat to this gift—tolerance cannot tolerate religions of intolerance and violence.

GIFT 22

Boston Tea Party. Who wants to pay taxes without having a voice in how the money is spent? Who wants to protest unconstitutional laws and have their protests contemptuously dismissed by their government? Who wants to be cheated by unfair trade practices and feel they can never get ahead? What will this mean for our children? What kind of future will they have? In the 18th century, British subjects in America asked these questions.

IT WAS A QUARREL that had gone on for years. Lack of affection and the unwillingness of some members of the 'family' to treat other members with respect lay at its root.

It was a big family, and like families everywhere some of the members had difficulty relating. They were divided by thousands of miles of ocean, and by quite different experiences.

Most of the free people in America were descended from British settlers. They were British subjects. They were passionate about the inheritance of liberty and self-government, which they had received from their forebears. People who arrived from other countries shared their love of freedom. When their right to govern themselves was denied, they rebelled. The American War of Independence began as a British civil war.

During the Glorious Revolution of 1688/1689, a convention of the British people negotiated the Declaration of Rights with new rulers. In December 1689, Parliament enacted the Declaration as the Bill of Rights.

The Bill of Rights restated ancient rights—the right to bear arms, to be represented in Parliament, to have the right to trial by jury and to be free of the rule of foreign states and potentates. Taxes were to be approved by the people's representatives.

Arbitrary prosecutions and cruel punishments were forbidden. The Glorious Revolution inspired the American Revolution.

In 1773, Americans were angered that Parliament had given a British firm, the East India Company, a tea concession that allowed it to undersell American competitors. They were furious about paying a tax on the tea because they had no part in approving the tax. And they were outraged that Parliament planned to use the tax to pay the salaries of colonial governors. This made the governors dependent on Parliament rather than accountable to the colonial assemblies, which traditionally had paid their salaries.

Americans in three ports refused to unload the tea, and sent the ships back to Britain. In Boston, they dropped 342 chests of tea into the harbour, to steep in the water.

The family in London—though not all of them, many were sympathetic—responded with fury. George III and Parliament imposed the Coercion Acts—they were renamed the Intolerable Acts by Americans. Boston Harbour was blockaded until the cost of the spoiled tea was paid. The whole of Massachusetts was placed under martial law.

Men such as Sam Adams, John Adams, George Washington, John Jay and Benjamin Franklin protested, but to no avail. Franklin published his sardonic *Rules By Which A Great Empire May Be Reduced to A Small One* to point out that the actions of King and Parliament were self-defeating. Indignant New Yorkers wrote to the Mayor of London, *We are born to the bright inheritance of English freedom.* George Washington wrote a friend, *The Parliament of Great Britain have no more right to put their hands into my pocket, without my consent, than I have to put my hands into yours for money.*

The people of the thirteen American colonies—though not all of them, some supported Parliament and King—demanded their rights under the British Constitution. They published protests in newspapers and sent out circulars. In July 1774, Fairfax County, Virginia, declared—

That the most important and valuable part of the British constitution, upon which its very existence depends, is the fundamental principle of the people's being governed by no laws to which they have not given their consent, by representatives freely chosen by themselves who are affected by the laws they enact equally with their constituents, to whom they are accountable, and whose burthens they share, in which consists the safety and happiness of the community...

For the first time, elected representatives from twelve of the thirteen colonies met together. In September 1774, they held the First Continental Congress in Philadelphia.

In Williamsburg, the irate Governor of Virginia dissolved the rebellious House of Burgesses. They moved their session to Raleigh Tavern.

One hundred years earlier, in the 1680s, English doctor John Locke had secretly written *Two Treatises of Civil Government* and *A Letter Concerning Toleration.* One hundred years later his work was still being read in America. Doctor Locke diagnosed four ills in society and prescribed four cures—

1. We have a right to freedom of conscience.
2. We have a right to own, sell, bequeath and transfer our property.
3. Our government must be based on our popular consent.
4. We have the right to rebel when government does not protect our life, liberty and property.

In America they took Locke seriously. They asserted that they had been denied their natural rights and that they had a right to do something about it. Congress organized a trade boycott, pledged to go to the aid of Massachusetts if the colony were to be attacked, and sent another message to the King pleading for justice. Their appeal hit a brick wall.

Boston remained under armed guard and languished for lack of trade. Americans began to drum new life into their militias.

John Locke was an outstanding political and social philosopher. He was a liberal at a time when liberals believed in freedom and limited government.

Parliament ordered the Royal Governor of Massachusetts to destroy the Americans' arms depot in the village of Concord so they could not defend themselves. Doctor Joseph Warren learned of the secret plan, and sent riders to sound the alarm. Church bells pealed and bonfires were lit, calling local militias into action.

Lexington farmer and minuteman, John Parker

At dawn on April 19th 1775, fifty armed minutemen faced hundreds of British soldiers on Lexington Green. The youngest American was 18. The oldest was 63. The British commanding officer shouted, *Lay down your arms, you damned rebels, or you are all dead men.* They refused.

It is not clear who fired first. Eight Lexington men were killed. Militiamen from surrounding villages fought back at Concord's North Bridge and from behind barns, stonewalls and trees. News of the conflict ran like a fire through the colonies.

The Second Continental Congress met and elected George Washington commander of the forces for the defence of liberty. He took the mission, but refused to take a salary. He was about to face the most powerful army in the world.

George Washington's family was of English descent, and he had supported the British Army as a Colonel when he was a young man. Initially he regarded conflict between the American colonies and the British King as a tragedy. But Washington and his fellow Americans became willing to die for an important truth that they saw—they had to be free to live their lives.

Washington *dispenses happiness around him*, wrote a friend. Strong enough to lift a man in each hand, Washington was fearless in battle and was devoted to his soldiers. He had the foresight to save his men from disease by having them inoculated against smallpox. He engineered miraculous escapes and learned from his defeats—and there were many of them. When he succeeded, he was glad to acknowledge and honour the help of Providence and the contributions of the soldiers and officers fighting with him.

Washington inspired men and women with his audacity and honesty. His fortitude was legendary.

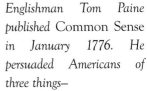

Englishman Tom Paine published Common Sense *in January 1776. He persuaded Americans of three things—*

A hereditary king is a bad thing. There is a difference between a willful attack and unavoidable defence. Posterity would welcome an independent republic where free citizens ruled themselves and helped to create 'peace for ever'.

On July 4th 1776, the Continental Congress approved the Declaration of Independence. Bells rang, bonfires were lit and statues of the king were pulled down.

I shall constantly bear in mind that as the sword was the last resort for the preservation of our liberties, so it ought to be the first to be laid aside when those liberties are firmly established.

—George Washington

Americans declared independence in 1776. They were defending gifts, which generations of British people had given them.

The following account of the men and women who dared to win freedom in the American Revolution will resonate with anyone who has also dared and endured.

On August 27th 1776, the King's troops prepared to deliver a fatal defeat to the American army on Long Island. Two American regiments had given their lives to buy time for a retreat, but Washington and the American Army were trapped against the East River.

Then, within hours, scores of little boats slipped out from Manhattan and across the river, silently picking up 9,000 of their fellow Americans and rowing them to safety. Strong winds providentially kept the Royal Navy away. A morning fog shrouded the last men to leave. Washington stepped into the last boat.

In the autumn, after suffering a series of devastating defeats, Washington's dwindling army fled from Manhattan through New Jersey and across the Delaware River into Pennsylvania.

By Christmas 1776, the American army was in tatters, hungry and demoralized. Thousands of soldiers had gone home. Those who remained were planning to leave at the end of December when their enlistments ended. Then reinforcements arrived, and Washington asked them to stay for one last attempt. He had Thomas Paine's *Crisis* read to them—

> *These are the times that test men's souls. The summer soldier and the sunshine patriot will, in this crisis, shrink from the service of their country; but he that stands by it now, deserves the love and thanks of man and woman. Tyranny, like hell, is not easily conquered; yet we have this consolation with us, that the harder the conflict, the more glorious the triumph.*

Nation Makers

Late on Christmas Day, they followed Washington back across the Delaware in a violent snowstorm, marching for nine miles—some of them barefoot—to reach Trenton where they surprised and captured 1,000 Hessians, the King's German mercenaries. On January 2nd 1777, pursued by the King's troops, who followed them by the marks their bloody feet left in the snow, they marched on Princeton.

The advance guard of Americans was attacked, and fell back. Washington spurred his horse into a fast gallop, waving his hat and calling his men forward, and raced straight toward the King's troops who lifted their muskets and fired. Washington disappeared in the smoke. He emerged to lead the capture of Princeton.

Washington pursued a strategy of retreat, evade and strike. Starving winters, a weak and feckless Congress

Freedom-loving Brits opposed sending troops to suppress the American rebellion. It was an unpopular war in Britain. In Parliament William Pitt cried, 'The Americans are the sons, not the bastards, of England'.

Widows and wives joined the American Army. They served as laundresses, cooks and nurses and searched for abandoned munitions on battlefields. Thousands of women 'held the fort' —managing farms and businesses at home while their husbands and fathers were in the field.

Americans received outside help from the French and Dutch governments and from many individuals.

I will not...despair.

   —*George Washington*

❀

Valley Forge, Pennsylvania. During the winter of 1778, each cabin housed twelve men, many of them without blankets. Washington's wife Martha, his strongest supporter, came north from Mount Vernon every winter to tend the ill.

American Army Camp at Valley Forge.

and financial speculators—Washington called them *that host of infamous harpies*—almost defeated Americans.

The war was fought from Montreal, Canada, in the north, to Savannah, Georgia, in the south. In 1775 Ethan Allen and the Green Mountain Boys had captured Fort Ticonderoga in upstate New York. Later that year, bookseller Henry Knox and his men dragged 60 tons of artillery 300 snowy miles from the fort to Boston to give Americans armaments. In 1776, British General Burgoyne marched south from Canada, to cut off New England, and one thousand axe-men felled trees and bridges to make his road a *labyrinthine hell.* Meanwhile General Stark and the New Hampshire militia pummeled Burgoyne's troops.

Not all victories were obtained in battle. The keys to holding West Point were the fortifications designed by engineer Tadeusz Kosciuszko.

On September 11th 1777, a combined total of almost 30,000 British and American troops fought one another at the Battle of Brandywine in Pennsylvania. The American

Revolution's most indispensable men—George Washington, Alexander Hamilton, the Marquis de Lafayette and General Nathanael Greene—barely escaped death or capture.

Washington was saved by British chivalry. Before the battle, he rode out to view the terrain. A British marksman with a repeating rifle had him in his sights, but held his fire. Patrick Ferguson later wrote, *It was not pleasant to fire at the back of an unoffending individual who was acquitting himself coolly of his duty* . . .

Faulty intelligence almost defeated the outnumbered Americans. Near Birmingham Friends Meeting House the King's army surprised and outflanked them. Several divisions resisted valiantly, and sustained heavy losses. Lafayette fought while a wound filled his boot with blood.

Washington and Greene arrived with reinforcements and positioned their men to hold off the King's divisions. As Hessian mercenaries drove across the Brandywine, overrunning the artillery, and Americans fell back, fighting hand-to-hand across the fields and hills, George Weedon and his Virginians stood that sweltering September afternoon and fought, withdrew and stood and fought again. Their fighting withdrawal bought time for the American army. Darkness fell, and Count Casimir Pulaski, at the head of the cavalry, covered the American escape to Chester.

Much of the American artillery was lost, but not all of it. Edward Hector, in an action of outstanding bravery, rescued a number of cannon in the face of the Hessian advance. The wounded on both sides were cared for under flags of truce. Some of the British and American dead were buried together at Birmingham Meeting House.

As the war entered its sixth year, Daniel Morgan won a brilliant victory at Cowpens, South Carolina. Nathanael Greene led the daring strategy that freed the South and sent General Cornwallis and the forces

Throughout the war years, Washington gave a part of every day to private prayer, often going to a grove of trees to be alone. He wrote, 'No man has a more perfect reliance on the all-wise and powerful dispensations of the Supreme Being than I have, nor thinks His aid more necessary'.

❋

Inspired by freedom and equality of opportunity, millions of people from all over the world have come to America to create a new life.

of the King reeling north. Lafayette, whom Washington had come to love like a son, stopped Cornwallis and penned his forces in Yorktown. The French Navy prevented their escape after a storm incapacitated the Royal Navy. Washington, bringing his army secretly south in one final surprise, defeated the enemies of independence at Yorktown in 1781. The British surrendered as their fife-and-drum corps played 'The World Turned Upside Down'.

British armies left America in 1783. Washington amazed and awed the courts of Europe, which expected him to seize power. Instead, he resigned his army commission, and on Christmas Eve 1783 rode home to Mount Vernon.

GIFT 22

Governments Derive Their Just Powers From Our Consent. Whenever Any Government becomes Destructive of Our Rights and Liberties, We Have the Right to Alter or Abolish It.

The American Revolution confirms that resisting injustice can be painful. The goal that made it worthwhile was establishing a representative government with the blessings of liberty. But could that be done?

GIFTS 23 & 24

Independence Hall, Philadelphia. In 1787, four years after the war had ended, many feared that America's weak national government would be blown away. In Washington's words, *it was shaken to its foundation, and liable to be overset by every blast.*

CONCERNED CITIZENS decided to act. During the sultry summer of 1787, delegates from twelve of the thirteen new states met in Independence Hall to draft a constitution that would set forth government's guiding principles and organization. They grappled with creating a national government that had scope for action but never so much power that it became despotic.

They were lawyers and judges, a brilliant entrepreneur, an inventor, at least two farmers and seven governors. They ranged in age from men in their thirties to Benjamin Franklin, who was 81. Thirty of the fifty-five men had been officers under Washington's command in the war. They elected Washington to serve as president of the convention.

John Adams, working feverishly in London, had sent delegates his thoughts on various constitutions. He called Britain's Constitution *the greatest fabric of invention in human history.* He noted that it had established three branches of government.

When those branches were working, they balanced each other and prevented king, parliament or judges from becoming too powerful.

The relationship between the Courts, Monarch, Parliament and People is described in the institutions and founding documents of the British Constitution:

1. Common Law
2. Monarch & Coronation Oath
3. Magna Carta
4. Parliament
5. Declaration of Rights/Bill of Rights

To create a responsive government that protected liberty and opportunity, American delegates built on the old and created a new constitution.

You might think of the structure of the oak tree as a visual sketch of the British and US Constitutions.

The 'Earth' is the people's birthright of freedom.

The 'roots' of the tree are the people and their free economy, local communities, local governments, sheriffs, schools and fire departments. Like the roots of a tree these are often unseen and unappreciated, but they are vital to our lives.

Just law is the supporting 'trunk'.

The main 'branches' are the legislature (Parliament or Congress), the executive (the Sovereign or President) and the judiciary (courts of justice under Common Law). If one branch becomes too big and powerful, it can topple the tree.

The 'Sun' is the divine or universal ideal, which gives illumination to the people.

The people and their freedom nourish the Constitution, and are nourished by it.

The British Constitution influenced the French philosopher Montesquieu. In his Spirit of the Laws *(1748), he advocated the separation of powers, the preservation of civil liberties and the rule of law. In turn he influenced American thinking by calling for a government so constructed that 'no man need be afraid of another'.*

The convention process respected listening. The delegates addressed their comments to Washington (not to each other) and spoke only twice on the same issue. Washington rarely spoke.

Freedom of speech knows no political station, no power structure nor race, colour or creed.

–The Senate of Canada

A phrase of astonishing simplicity, heard for the first time in the history of the world in 1787: *We the People... We the People in order to form a more perfect union, establish justice, insure domestic tranquility, provide for the common defense, promote the general welfare, and secure the Blessings of Liberty to ourselves and our posterity, do ordain and establish this Constitution for the United States of America.*

In order to secure 'the unalienable rights of life, liberty and the pursuit of happiness', only limited powers and specific responsibilities were given to the Federal Government. The states and the people retained many powers and responsibilities.

Power was balanced, separated, divided, and distributed. No branch of the government could fully function without the others; at the same time, each branch was to have a certain amount of autonomy.... And just as the oak drops old leaves and forms new buds and leaves, elected representatives of the people retire and new representatives are voted in.

To the Celtic people of the islands the oak tree was the gateway between worlds. Robin Hood's greenwood tree was the oak. In 1549 Robert Kett fought to preserve common lands for the people under the Oak of Reformation. In 1687, Connecticut's Charter was kept safe from destruction in the Charter Oak. In 1787 three Williams—Wilberforce, Pitt and Grenville—met under an oak tree, and swore to abolish the slave trade.

GIFT 23

A Limited and Representative Government Organized into Three Branches—Legislature, Executive, and Judiciary—under a Constitution and Just Law.

American soldiers and public officials do not swear to support and defend the President or Congress. They swear to support and defend the Constitution of the United States.

Inspired by the American experiment, Mozart and friends promoted the cause of liberty in Vienna. In The Marriage of Figaro, the composer gloriously supported the ideal of equality.

The US Constitution did not avoid a deadly flaw, and it omitted something critically important—a Bill of Rights that would codify and protect the natural rights and liberties of the people. Many of those liberties had been fought for in Britain over the course of a thousand years. They were part of the British Constitution. They included—

> *The freedom to own and sell property; the right to habeas corpus and to trial by jury; the right not to be fined excessively or punished cruelly; the right to be silent under interrogation; the right to your property and house, free of government searches or seizure—'your home is your castle'; the right to petition your government; the right not to have soldiers quartered in your house; the right to bear arms.*

Freedom-loving Americans insisted that the new Constitution be amended with a Bill of Rights. Ten amendments were debated and eventually ratified in state conventions, and the Bill of Rights came into effect on December 15th 1791.

Freedom of religion and freedom of speech became part of the Bill of Rights. The 10th Amendment wisely reserved all the powers not specifically delegated to the federal government to the states or the people.

The creators of the US Constitution and Bill of Rights wanted to support the creativity and strength of free people and local governments. They opposed the creeping menace of centralized power, no matter how seemingly beneficent.

Unlike central planners, they understood that freedom and responsibility help people become prosperous and that government must be limited in size and power. As Thomas Jefferson explained, under Article I, Section 8, *Congress does not have unlimited powers to provide for the general welfare, but [is] restrained to those specifically enumerated.* If the power to legislate on behalf of the 'general welfare' were unlimited, the power of Congress would be unlimited—a deadly recipe for disaster.

The individual right to bear arms, which is protected by the 2nd Amendment, frightens some people.

We hope that criminals will not target us and that arguments can be worked out peacefully. We would like to think that if someone attacked us, the police would arrive in time to protect us. Perhaps they would. But what if our own government attacked us?

Every genocide of the last one hundred years was committed against unarmed people by their own governments. Fifty-six million Russians, Chinese, Jews, Ottoman Empire Armenians, Cambodians, Vietnamese and Darfurians were disarmed and murdered. 'That could never happen here' is not a concept supported by history. When guns are outlawed, only outlaws—or governments—are armed.

The right to bear arms is intended to do one essential thing—protect the weak from the strong and violent. To shield children and innocents against assault, men and women have learned how to use arms responsibly.

The right of citizens to bear arms, said US Senator Hubert Humphrey, *is just one guarantee against arbitrary government, one more safeguard, against the tyranny, which now appears remote...but which historically has proven to be always possible.*

How wonderful it would be if the peoples of Earth could live freely and safely without being attacked!

The right of self-defense is the first law of nature...

—*St. George Tucker*

When seconds count, the police are only minutes away.

—*Author unknown*

Both oligarch and tyrant mistrust the people, and therefore deprive them of arms.

—*Aristotle*

Why do you think they disarmed slaves? Because if slaves had been armed, that would have been the end of slavery.

—*Thomas Sowell*

GIFT 24

THE FIRST TEN AMENDMENTS
TO THE U.S. CONSTITUTION—
THE BILL OF RIGHTS

¤ 1st Amendment: Congress shall make no law respecting an establishment of religion, or prohibiting the free exercise thereof; or abridging the freedom of speech, or of the press; or the right of the people peaceably to assemble, and to petition the Government for a redress of grievances.

¤ 2nd Amendment: A well-regulated Militia, being necessary to the security of a free State, the right of the people to keep and bear Arms, shall not be infringed.

¤ 3rd Amendment: No Soldier shall, in time of peace be quartered in any house, without the consent of the Owner, nor in time of war, but in a manner to be prescribed by law.

¤ 4th Amendment: The right of the people to be secure in their persons, houses, papers, and effects, against unreasonable searches and seizures, shall not be violated, and no Warrants shall issue, but upon probable cause, supported by Oath or affirmation, and particularly describing the place to be searched, and the persons or things to be seized.

¤ 5th Amendment: No person shall be held to answer for a capital, or otherwise infamous crime, unless on a presentment or indictment of a Grand Jury, except in cases arising in the land or naval forces, or in the Militia, when in actual service in time of War or public danger; nor shall any person be subject for the same offence to be twice put in jeopardy of life or limb, nor shall be compelled in any criminal case to be a witness against himself, nor be deprived of life, liberty, or property, without due process of law; nor shall private property be taken for public use without just compensation.

- ¤ 6th Amendment: In all criminal prosecutions, the accused shall enjoy the right to a speedy and public trial, by an impartial jury of the State and district wherein the crime shall have been committed; which district shall have been previously ascertained by law, and to be informed of the nature and cause of the accusation; to be confronted with the witnesses against him; to have compulsory process for obtaining witnesses in his favor, and to have the assistance of counsel for his defense.

- ¤ 7th Amendment: In Suits at common law, where the value in controversy shall exceed twenty dollars, the right of trial by jury shall be preserved, and no fact tried by a jury shall be otherwise re-examined in any Court of the United States, than according to the rules of the common law.

- ¤ 8th Amendment: Excessive bail shall not be required, nor excessive fines imposed, nor cruel and unusual punishments inflicted.

- ¤ 9th Amendment: The enumeration in the Constitution of certain rights shall not be construed to deny or disparage others retained by the people.

- ¤ 10th Amendment: The powers not delegated to the United States by the Constitution, nor prohibited by it to the States, are reserved to the States respectively, or to the people.

The freedoms in the Bill of Rights are a precious gift, but at first they were only available to some.

GIFT 25

In the history of the world, people of every colour have committed the outrage of enslaving men and women.

IN ENGLAND slavery had been abolished in 1102 (Gift 12). In the 18th century, a fellowship of Christians—men and women, white and black, young and old—fought to abolish the trans-Atlantic slave trade, and slavery in all British colonies.

I have a dream that my four little children will one day live in a nation where they will not be judged by the color of their skin but by the content of their character.

—The Reverend Martin Luther King

They included: Sir Charles Middleton, the brilliant naval officer who reformed the Royal Navy; his wife, Lady Middleton, a painter; James Ramsay, a surgeon who described the appalling treatment of slaves on Caribbean plantations; and members of the Society of Friends. William Wilberforce, an indomitable MP, led the struggle in Parliament. Thomas Clarkson learned about the horror of slavery while a student and rode thousands of miles all over England to awaken the public. John Newton, a former slave trader, wrote "Amazing Grace" and became an abolitionist. Olaudah Equiano, an audacious former slave and sailor, wrote an autobiography that revealed the infamy of slavery and the humanity of the slave. They contributed to a gift that had been spoken of for two thousand years, but had been missing from human history for most of that time.

At first the fellowship was small and made little headway. But the members persevered until their message became a great cause. After defeating Napoleon's planned invasion, the people of Britain gathered in mass meetings to oppose the slave trade, and flooded Parliament with petitions.

In 1807, as tears streamed down William Wilberforce's face, Parliament abolished the slave trade, and sent the Royal Navy into action.

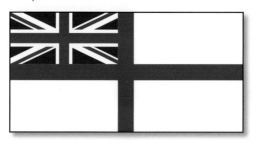

The Royal Navy was given the mission of stopping the slave trade. At great cost in sailors and soldiers killed and wounded, the Navy succeeded.

Although the trade had ended, the slaves already on the plantations of the Caribbean remained bound, and their children were born into servitude. The fellowship regrouped, and began a decades-long push to abolish slavery completely.

Women launched a large-scale boycott of sugar to pressure slave owners, and slaves rose desperately and bravely in a series of rebellions. They won a great victory when Parliament ended slavery throughout the British Empire in 1833—the first time any empire had done so. During the U.S. Civil War (1861-1865), President Abraham Lincoln emancipated American slaves. The promise of the Constitution and the Bill of Rights was being fulfilled.

Let us not pray that God is on our side in a war or any other time, but let us pray that we are on God's side.

Olaudah Equiano loved the Inheritance, and he knew that slavery would kill it —not only for slaves, for everyone. 'Surely this traffic cannot be good, which spreads like a pestilence, and taints what it touches!'

HMS Black Joke was a slave ship captured by the Royal Navy. She had a brilliant naval career pursuing slave ships and freeing slaves.

A musician and self-taught lawyer, Granville Sharp successfully fought for the Common Law principle that since every man and woman in England was free, any person brought to England as a slave was free and could not be returned to servitude. Sharp's large, musical family supported his campaign to abolish the slave trade.

Loathing slavery, George Washington freed his slaves and set aside a trust fund for them in his will.

A country's success depends on women.

For more than two thousand years, women in the islands led men in battle, managed farms, breweries, and forges, served as midwives and teachers, worked as bailiffs and merchants, built businesses and endowed schools, hospitals and colleges. They earned a living as artisans, performed on stage, wrote popular novels, composed music, healed the sick and helped to reform health care.

They became scientists, Sovereign Queens, MPs and a Prime Minister. They were the mother-half of the human race and they raised and defended children.

Tall and red-haired, Boudicca led her people against the Romans in AD 60 when they broke their treaty and raped her daughters. In the 10th century, the Lady of the Mercians, Aethelflaed, daughter of Alfred, defended her people from Viking marauders.

In 1588, when the Spanish Armada sailed into the Channel to invade England, Elizabeth I rode to Tilbury and declared to her soldiers, *I have come amongst you being resolved in the midst and heat of the battle to live or die amongst you all...* The Armada was defeated. The Virgin Queen encouraged global exploration. Virginia is named after her.

Women of the islands were remarkable writers. In the 14th century, Lady Julian of Norwich wrote *Revelations of Divine Love* to share her visions of God as Lord of courage, comfort and grace. Her book is still in print. In the early 19th century, Jane Austen published sparkling and enduringly popular classics. The importance of self-knowledge, a warm heart and right conduct play an intriguing role in her novels.

In the 20th century, Beatrix Potter wrote animal stories for children and used the profits to purchase 4,000 acres in the Lake District for a public park. In the 21st century, novelist Doris Lessing was awarded the Nobel Prize for literature, and JK Rowling became a billionaire and a favorite of children for her Harry Potter series. The phenomenal success of women points to the next gift.

One of the first fishing manuals was written by Dame Juliana Berners and published as part of the Boke of St. Albans in 1496.

It is our choices, Harry, that show what we truly are, far more than our abilities.

—JK Rowling

The love and respect of her father and mother contributes to a woman's success.

Eglantyne Jebb launched a campaign to bring supplies to the destitute children of Europe after the First World War, and founded Save the Children.

In the 19th century, Florence Nightingale—the lady with the lamp—courageously defied government bureaucracy, epidemics and battles to nurse soldiers in the Crimean War. Afterwards, Nightingale used what she had learned to reform health care. Mary Seacole was a successful innkeeper in Jamaica who left the Caribbean for the battlefields of Crimea. Her tenderness and courage as a nurse became a by-word among British troops.

The best shot in the Special Operations Executive (SOE), Violette Bushell Szabo was one of the women agents who parachuted into France to fight the Nazis during the Second World War. Taken prisoner, she was tortured but refused to betray the Resistance and was executed at Ravensbrück concentration camp.

Women won the right to vote in national elections in the Isle of Man in 1880-81; in New Zealand, 1893; in Australia, 1898; in Britain, 1918; and in the U.S. in 1920. It was high time.

Emmeline Pankhurst's fortitude when unjustly imprisoned, her eloquence and her visionary leadership of the Suffragettes won British women the right to vote in the 20th century. All men had won the right to vote and the secret ballot in the 19th century.

Edith Cavell started a nursing school in Belgium. When the First World War erupted, she cared for wounded Allied soldiers and helped them to escape. *Had I not, they would have been shot,* she said before she was executed by the German Army.

Between the 1940s and 1960s, Dorothy Hodgkin used X-ray crystallography to determine the structure of biomolecules. Her discoveries made possible the mass production of synthetic penicillin, insulin, and vitamin B12.

Margaret Thatcher became Britain's first woman Prime Minister. She helped to liberate the peoples of Eastern Europe from Soviet oppression and defended the Falkland Islanders from conquest. She believed in individual responsibility and tried to remove the dead hand of the state from Britain's economy.

No nation that suppresses and subjugates half its people is likely to succeed. In parts of the world, sickening attacks continue to be made against children and women, but in the most prosperous countries on Earth, children are protected and educated and women are the free equals of men.

Equality was a goal of abolitionists and suffragettes, but what does equality mean? Sports offer an interesting insight.

In the 18th and the 19th centuries, the people of the islands had established the rules for eight popular

Teaching girls and boys how to think for themselves is crucial. Children need individual attention and inspiration from caring, creative teachers in a safe place. They and their parents need 'the long-term benefits of school choice'.

Rugby player. Athletes don't expect or want equality of outcome, but they expect equality of opportunity under fair rules.

❀

The 14th Amendment to the U.S. Constitution affirmed every citizen had fundamental rights and liberties and equal protection under the law. Equal rights and protections are crucial to equality of opportunity.

❀

Be that thou know'st thou art, and then thou art as great as that thou fear'st.

—Shakespeare

The joy and glory of sports are grounded in fair play.

sports—football (soccer), rugby, golf, cricket, tennis, boxing, badminton and table tennis. They are fans of fair play. Why should anyone stand heartbroken behind a colour barrier?

To be passionate about fair play is to want fair play *for everyone*. Fair play means that each of us has the right to compete freely for a job, marry our beloved, buy a house, create a business, play sports, stand for office and vote. That is what fairness and equality mean. A constitutional government under just laws protects our opportunities. It does not guarantee our outcomes.

We can't be guaranteed equality of outcome since each of us has different talents and goals, but we must be treated fairly and justly. The jewel of dignity inside each of us makes us equals, and the spirit of understanding helps us to see and rejoice in that truth.

GIFT 25
All People Are Created Equal with Certain Unalienable Rights.

GIFT 26

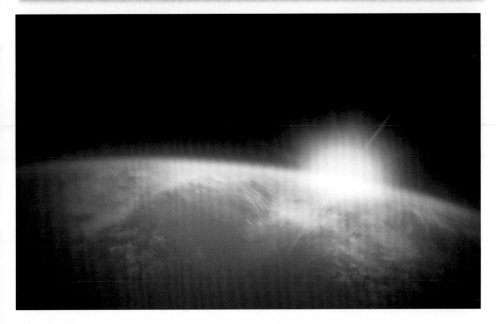

People who believe they can steer the world—its government, climate and economy—have been deluded by *the myth of power*. Biologist Gregory Bateson and philosopher Friedrich Hayek understood that *the myth of power* leads to disaster, for power destroys both freedom and knowledge. The shared knowledge and achievements of free men and women created the next gift.

ONE FROZEN NIGHT in December 1598, players and carpenters arrived at a London theatre carrying hooded lanterns, saws, hammers and chisels. Once inside, they began prising apart the oak boards of the stage, walls and floors.

They had taken matters into their own hands because the man who owned the land under the theatre claimed that the building was his with the end of their lease, which he refused to renew. He shut them out of the theatre they had built.

At dawn the neighbourhood woke up to the exploit—the actors had taken their play-house apart timber by timber and carried it across the Thames to Bankside where they rebuilt it as the Globe.

Shakespeare was one of the players. Now that he had a theatre again he wrote *Much Ado About Nothing*, *Henry V*, *Julius Caesar*, *As You Like It*, *All's Well That Ends Well*, *King Lear*, *Macbeth*, *Hamlet*, *Antony and Cleopatra* and *the Tempest*. The bard was lucky. For

Managers and players like William Shakespeare shared expenses and profits. They were among the world's first shareholders. Shakespeare's reconstructed Globe Theatre mounts productions today.

For generations, fishermen successfully managed the fishing grounds around Britain as a common, shared resource.

centuries, men and women had created the freedom, property rights and economic success that made it possible for him to be a playwright. Otherwise, Shakespeare might have been a serf.

Property is a cold word until you realize it means your home, your photographs, your grandmother's vase and your child's paintings, your garden, your bed, your car and the food you eat. Your property is your hard work and ideas made real and visible in the world.

You've heard the famous story of the pencil, whose production involves people all over the globe. In a free economy we are connected to thousands of people near and far who help us to live—producing copper for the pipes that carry fresh water invisibly under our streets; growing wheat for our bread; manufacturing our clothes; building our furniture and homes—though not necessarily out of the goodness of their hearts.

It is not from the benevolence of the butcher, the brewer, or the baker, that we expect our dinner, wrote Adam Smith, *but from their regard to their own interest.* Born in Kirkcaldy, Adam Smith looked deep inside human beings. In *The Wealth of Nations,* published in London in 1776, he pointed out that most of us want the best for ourselves and that this trait is unlikely to change But Adam Smith saw we are also moved by sympathy.

When we have the freedom to make a living within a system of just laws we will cooperate with others, and our cooperation will be good for almost everybody.

The economy that Adam Smith described has been called capitalism. Smith never used the word—it was invented later—and it is misleading. We prefer the phrase the free economy—a people-created economy where we freely invent, manufacture, market, buy, sell, trade, invest, provide services and create purposeful work.

The inspiration and creative work that are part of a free economy cannot be reduced to the word capitalism.

Controlling an economy is an efficient way to dominate people. Power-hungry operators have imposed communism, national socialism and fascism on their hapless peoples in order to subjugate and exploit them. They ruined economies and millions of human beings. In contrast, the free economy *has lifted hundreds of millions of people out of poverty*, and enhanced their lives.

Creating the free economy requires courage and imagination. Men and women have to oppose injustice and establish and defend fair laws and wages. They have to battle monopolies and big government-big business cronyism. They have to reduce heavy taxes and tariffs, eliminate corruption and withering regulations and protect their water, air and earth. Businesses have the challenge of surviving, making a profit and being fair to their employees. It's a tall order, as history suggests.

Adam Smith in Chengdu, China. He understood that the decisions of millions of individuals, acting out of self-interest and empathy with others, guided the free economy. He knew that prosperity depended on people acting ethically. He had the endearing habit of giving his salary to those in need.

❀

. . . some work preserves the household of life, and some work destroys it.

—Wendell Berry

Vancouver, BC. Advances in agriculture, sanitation and medicine meant most British babies were growing up. Brits began to explore and trade globally. They helped to build America, Canada, Australia, New Zealand, India, Singapore and Hong Kong.

Chaucer's pilgrims rode to Canterbury in the 1380s, the same decade that the free men of the Great Rising marched on London. The pilgrims included a carpenter, weaver, ploughman, cook, miller and yeoman forester. Any of them might have joined the revolt.

Medieval England was not a peasant society where land was collectively owned by families and rarely sold. Instead, men and women bought and sold land frequently—and revolted against oppressive government.

In 1381, free men mounted a fierce resistance to a poll tax, lower wages and vile efforts to turn them back into serfs. Sending *messengers carrying letters and instructions from village to village*, they marched on London. The young Richard II betrayed them, but the poll tax was scuttled and serfdom disappeared. The new thinking supported an individual's right to freely negotiate wages.

From the 14th, to 17th centuries, travellers commented on the wealth of the English—*They eat plentifully of fish and flesh, live in comfortable houses, drink beer or wine, wear fine wool and own a great store of tools.* Montesquieu attributed their prosperity to liberty and independence. Low taxes, Common Law and team spirit all contributed.

The Industrial Revolution ultimately improved life, but it generated terrible challenges. There was degrading poverty, some of it the result of greed and the abandonment of ethics.

In 1824, Parliament had repealed the Combination Act, which prohibited trade unions and collective wage bargaining, but in 1825 Parliament declared new restrictions. In 1832, the Tolpuddle Martyrs tried to bargain collectively for better wages, and were punished by being transported to Australia. Outraged islanders protested, and eventually freed them. Subsequent decades would see match girls, mill workers and coal miners organizing to obtain living wages.

In the 1840s, tariffs created by the Corn Laws distorted the free market. Families could not afford bread. In 1846, after a popular campaign, Parliament repealed the Corn Laws, and released an unforeseen tide of prosperity.

In a free economy, people exercise the right to free association by forming partnerships and shareholder corporations. The government does not tell them how to run their businesses or bail them out if they fail. The free economy supports *an evolutionary process* of competition, selection and adaptation. People who are poor frequently become prosperous, and they help others.

Over the centuries the islanders built grammar schools, hospitals, universities and charitable trusts. In the 19th century two men planted the seed of the Friendly Society, an *astonishing phenomenon* in Britain, America and Canada. Thousands of local Friendly Societies served as insurance and safety nets for millions of people in case of illness, unemployment or death.

Most advances came not from the government but from individual people working together—

> Almost the entire social order of the country arose from private initiatives. Schools, colleges and universities; municipalities, hospitals, theatres; festivals and even the army regiments, all tell the same story: some public-spirited amateur, raising funds, setting out principles, acquiring premises, and then bequeathing his [or her] achievement to trustees or to the Crown... Their attitude to officialdom reflected their conviction that, if something needs doing, then the person to do it is you.

—Roger Scruton

If the industrial nations really want to help the Africans, they should finally terminate this awful aid. Huge bureaucracies are financed; corruption and complacency are promoted, Africans are taught to be beggars and not to be independent.

—African economist
James Shikwati

To prosper we need property rights and entrepreneurs.

If people are neighborly, they need the state less.

—Glenn Reynolds

William Hogarth's campaign for copyright protection for visual artists during their lifetimes succeeded. He painted Chairing the MP in the 1750s.

Don't ask me what I want it for, if you don't wanna pay some more.

—George Harrison

Power tends to corrupt...

—Lord Acton

LADY GODIVA

Legendary Lady Godiva and Robin Hood were tax protestors. Lady Godiva opposed her husband's high taxes and accepted his challenge to ride naked through town. He cut taxes. Robin Hood took particular aim at rapacious taxmen. He liked to liberate tax money and return it to distressed taxpayers.

Governments, as Adam Smith observed, are expert at siphoning money from the pockets of the people. A government that takes initiative away from citizens by trying to handle every major decision for them ends up treating them like children and taxing them heavily. But citizens are not children. They have the demanding and transcendent destiny of becoming adults.

The free economy is based on a mutual covenant freely entered into—a promise from one person or set of people to provide services or goods and a promise from another person to provide payment. Those who promise falsely and break their covenant are rightly punished by the law and scorned. At its best this free and mutual covenant helps us to prosper.

Shortly after the Second World War, in the beautiful old countries of Eastern Europe, the people's free economies were destroyed. Backed by a violent foreign state, governments promised the people a world of security where all citizens would have everything they wanted—free health care, free education and a guaranteed job. They called this socialism. They said it was a moral imperative.

The question that these governments never answered was, what will this cost? The people liked the idea of security, and they were afraid—their new leaders were attacking business people and imprisoning dissenters.

Prague, a city of despair and irony under socialism.

They gave away their free economy and lost everything they had. There was nothing they had once loved, including happiness and self-respect, which they did not lose.

You saw their losses in their shabby clothes, the grey, unpainted buildings that had once been the colours of sorbet, the crumbling stone of their bridges, the dirtiness of their water and air and, looking down at your plate, the greasy, bad food. Most of all you saw their losses in their faces—in the angry, envious, desperate and ironic look in their eyes.

Ironic, because they were told all this was for their own good. They lived in countries where everyone worked for the state for an income that could barely support them, where what they earned was regularly taken from them, where their right to live in their home depended on the whim of bureaucrats, where no one started a new business and no one had much—except the 'elites', who wore fine clothes, drove expensive black cars with tinted windows and were backed up by guns and tanks.

In their hubris the 'elites' believed they could control the economy down to the last thumbtack. Instead they drove the economy into the ground because they lacked the real information and imaginative energy that could be provided only by people creating, buying and selling

The idea that political freedom can be preserved in the absence of economic freedom, and vice versa, is an illusion.

— Ludwig von Mises

Aesop's ancient tale of the greedy man who killed the goose that laid the golden eggs is retold when a greedy government uses the heavy axe of taxes on businesses that create jobs.

in a free and evolving economy. There was no transparency, no accountability, no flexibility and no rule by just law. As a result, grocery shelves were empty, electricity was fitful and cars cost the earth, but no one dared to protest. If they did, they were jailed.

The people lacked the incentives and creative choices of the free economy. Firms could not strive to outperform competitors by improving products and services or reducing costs, and individuals and families could not choose the products and services best for them. Instead, burdened with rules and regulations governing every aspect of their lives and impoverished by state rationing, they were oppressed and humiliated.

They were no longer on the road to serfdom. They had become serfs.

Of all their losses, perhaps the most painful was the loss of hope. They had no hope for themselves and no hope for their children. The moment when their child understood and became hopeless was most painful.

In Prague and in other East European cities and countries, the story had a happy ending. With a little help from freedom-loving allies in Britain and America, brave men and women rose up together and took their cities and countries back. They began to create free economies with liberty, just laws and hope.

Good government defends just laws and the free economy and protects the vulnerable. Rational government asks, *In this particular case, is government the solution or will government make the problem worse?* Inspired by his Christian faith, Lord Shaftesbury persuaded government that it must protect children from being exploited. Shaftesbury is remembered in Piccadilly Circus by Anteros, 'the god of love returned', releasing his shaft.

Intangible wealth helps to create a free economy. It is more valuable than resources or infrastructure in generating prosperity. Intangible wealth includes an honest and efficient judicial system; documented and protected property rights; effective, incorruptible government; education; ethical businesses that pay a fair wage; and trust between people. Intangible wealth helps to create a world where we want to live.

The free economy depends on intangible wealth, small government and all the free people who help to create it. In short, the free economy depends on you.

GIFT 26
The Free Economy under the Rule of Just Law.

A free economy depends on honesty the way our body depends on our feet.

The advance of human liberty can only strengthen the cause of world peace.

–US President Ronald Reagan

GIFT 27

You understood this gift when you were a child.

Love suffers long, and is kind; love is not jealous, does not brag and is not arrogant. Love is not rude, is not selfish, is not easily provoked, and does not brood over an injury. Love does not rejoice in injustice. Love rejoices in the truth. Love supports us, trusts and endures.

—St Paul

To laugh often
and love much;

to win...the affection
of children;

to earn the approbation
of honest citizens...

To appreciate beauty;
to find the best in others;
to give of one's self;

...to know even one life
has breathed easier
because you have lived.

THE GOLDEN RULE illuminates every gift. It is the measure by which they are measured. It is a guide for those who are searching, a comfort to the ill, refreshment for the young and weary, a hand that strengthens, a friendship that never fails, the flag of our souls. The infinite riches of the Golden Rule have their source in a humble, sometimes overlooked spiritual law—to bless another is to be blessed.

GIFT 27

Do Unto Others as You Would Have Them Do Unto You—

Treat Others as You Would Wish To Be Treated.

Never forget

Life asks us to respond.

WE REMEMBER that millions of men and women and children endured lives of misery and were murdered by tyrants and dictatorships. The self-obsessed despots who terrorized them built memorials to themselves. Happily, little that they built remains—

> ...Round the decay
> Of that colossal wreck, boundless and bare,
> The lone and level sands stretch far away...

In contrast, the Inheritance—a living masterpiece that belongs to us all—survives.

Cathedral Church of the Blessed Virgin Mary, Salisbury Cathedral.

The Inheritance inspired cathedrals. The flowering of Gothic architecture began in France.

The Ancient Greek word for truth meant not to forget.

Some have tried to denigrate the Inheritance and belittle the gifts, but most of us know better. Parents and children use the Inheritance to make wise decisions. Innovators and inventors draw on the Inheritance to make discoveries. Men and women build profitable, ethical businesses with the gifts. And citizens who understand the Inheritance refuse to entrust their lives and liberties to behemoth governments that suppress freedom and creativity.

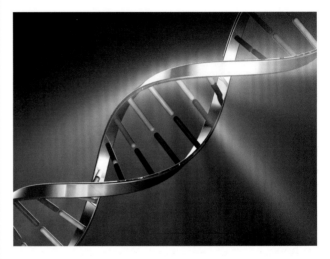

The Double Helix of DNA was discovered at Cambridge University. If all your DNA was *woven into a single fine strand, there would be enough...to stretch from the Earth to the Moon and back...again and again.*

Each of us has ten thousand trillion cells. In almost every one of our cells there are six-and-a-half feet of densely compressed strands of DNA.

The Inheritance is our spiritual, cultural and political DNA. Men and women helped to create its intricate power and grace. Imagine for a minute our world without the gifts of the Inheritance.

Newton by Blake

Imagine our world without affordable food and clothing, modern medicine or electric lights, without warm homes, clean water and paved roads.

Imagine our world without parks or schools, radio, television, phones, photographs, the Internet or most breeds of dogs and farm animals.

Imagine our world without jet planes, bicycles or trains, without refrigeration, insulin, antibiotics, painkillers, oxygen machines, artificial hips, ECGs, defibrillators, MRIs, CT scans or vaccinations against virulent disease.

Imagine our world without soccer, rugby, basketball, lawn tennis, table tennis, golf, cricket or fly-fishing, without the 3-note musical chord, stereophonic sound, English gardens or the Hubble Space Telescope.

Imagine a world where people in need are not cared for, where there are no helping hands, no trust and no hope, where piracy rages across the high seas and where wars against monstrous evil are lost.

Imagine a world where despots rule the Earth, a world without government of, by and for the people, without just laws that protect you, your family and your home.

The world you have been imagining is a world without the Inheritance. The islands are small. For many years they were sparsely populated. Yet when the islanders built on the Inheritance, they helped to invent almost every innovation we have named and many others. They explored and mapped the globe. One of them, Timothy Berners-Lee, formulated the worldwide web and gave it freely to all of us.

The Inheritance freed them to write—Chaucer, Shakespeare, John Donne, George Herbert, Milton, Defoe, Doctor Johnson, Robert Burns, Jane Austen, Blake, Keats, Dickens, George Eliot, Tennyson, Wordsworth, Hardy, Oscar Wilde, GK Chesterton, PG Wodehouse, George Orwell, JRR Tolkien, CS Lewis, Agatha Christie, JK Rowling…

Early creators of the Inheritance made the dog and cat our friends.

The people of the British Commonwealth and the United States entered the Second World War to prevent killers from killing. When they had overcome the Axis Powers, *they kept no territory beyond the graves where their soldiers lie.* When their defeated enemies were starving, the islanders made sacrifices to feed them, and Americans helped them to rebuild.

Charles Dickens spoke for us when he wrote—

> *In the little world in which children have their existence, ...there is nothing so finely perceived and so finely felt, as injustice.*

Men, women and children around the world want justice. We want freedom, wellbeing and peace. We want representative government, a free economy and honest leaders who respect the law and serve us. We want to be treated with dignity and to live in friendship and trust. We want to share intangible and tangible wealth. And we have a right to these gifts. The Inheritance is our birthright. When we look at the men and women who sacrificed to

The Mysterious Monument by John Constable. In the islands, the Inheritance sustained thousands of artists—Inigo Jones, Christopher Wren, Grinling Gibbons, Hogarth, 'Capability' Brown, Thomas Chippendale, the Adam Brothers, Gainsborough, George Stubbs, William Blake, Turner, AWN Pugin, Edward Burne-Jones, William Morris, Gertrude Jekyll, Edwin Lutyens, Henry Moore...

Lake District National Park, the Langdales. Here, Neolithic people polished stone axe heads and traded them across prehistoric Britain and Europe. Today, local people care for the park. We are called to protect both freedom and the Earth.

Fare well.

give us the Inheritance, we see how great we are and how wise, courageous and loving we are called to be.

Imagine if we lived in a world where everyone enjoyed and shared the gifts.

We are the defenders of the Inheritance.

Study Guide

The·Merry·Friar·carrieth·
Robin·acrofs·fhe·Water :·

*Here are the questions that occurred
to us as we studied the Inheritance.*

GIFT 3, pp. 7–9

Do you have a story about how a friend
has helped you, perhaps even saved
your life, and how you have helped a
friend?

GIFT 4, p. 10

Have you ever refused to obey an unjust or unfair order? What was that like
and what happened?

GIFTS 5 & 6, pp. 10–19

Which Celtic saints mentioned here
—or one you have heard about—do you
like best and why?

Have you ever forgiven someone or
been forgiven? How did you feel afterwards? Is your community grounded in
Judaeo-Christian ethics or some other
ethics? What are the ways we can treat
another person with dignity?

Do you see a connection between
having responsibility and being able to
respond? What responsibilities are you
glad to have, and what responsibilities
do you dislike?

THE SEVEN POWERS, p. 20

Which of the Seven Powers are you
happiest to have? If you don't possess
one of the Powers, how would you go
about getting it? How could the Seven
Powers help you to survive a personal or
national crisis?

GIFTS 7 & 8, pp. 21–28

Do you believe an elected leader
should be willing to die to defend his
people?

How do you depend on the law? Do
you believe that the same law should
apply to everyone? If yes, why? If people
follow traffic laws, is that a result of the
laws and the police or something else?

GIFT 9, pp. 21-28

What is the most important promise you have kept? What important promise has another person made to you, and kept?

Who do you trust? Why? Is trusting others important to your community?

LEADERSHIP LESSONS, pp. 26-27

Can you think of other leaders who have followed Alfred's leadership lessons? Can you see how Alfred's kind of leadership might be used in a business? How would a business leader serve rather than boss his employees? What might be the result? How would you use Alfred's leadership lessons in your life?

GIFT 10, pp. 29-32

What would a leader need to do to keep his or her covenant with you? What action would make you feel he or she had broken covenant with you? How would that feel? What would you do?

GIFT 11, pp. 32-35

How many countries in the world have leaders who have placed themselves above the law?

GIFT 12, pp. 35-37

Why do you think Anselm loved freedom? Do you think slavery is repugnant? Why? What would you do if you were a slave?

GIFTS 13 & 14, pp. 37-52

What do you think of the Code of Chivalry? Is it an antiquated idea? If not, why not? Does chivalry only belong to men? Did chivalry have anything to do with the establishment of Magna Carta?

Have you ever been treated unjustly? What are some effective ways to respond?

Have you experienced Christian contemplation?

The people who established Magna Carta were young, middle-aged and older, English, Welsh and Scots, bishops, knights and barons, townspeople and country people. What motivated them? Which of the rights in Magna Carta do you find personally significant? Why is Magna Carta still important today?

GIFT 15, p. 53

Many people share a number of common resources—clean water, for instance. What common resources do you share and how are they cared for?

GIFT 16, pp. 54-60

What inspired the Montforts to risk their lives? Did they fear death? Why is being willing to risk your life sometimes essential to living?

Why was founding a parliament important? How does establishing parliament relate to Gifts 10 & 11—the covenant between leader and people and the principle that not even the king is above the law? What is the most powerful tool that a parliament or congress has when trying to control the power of a modern prime minister or president? How responsive is your parliament or congress?

GIFT 17, pp. 61–65

Why were Christians receptive to scientific discovery? When were they not receptive? Have you seen availability bias or reputation cascade affecting the news and you?

GIFT 18, pp. 65–67

Peace and generosity were crucial to this gift. How has the generosity of someone else changed your life for the better? How has your generosity changed someone else's life?

GIFTS 19, 20 & 21, pp. 68–78

John and Elizabeth Lilburne based the right to silence on the human dignity of every person. Why is that right still important today?

William Penn helped to establish the principle that a jury has a right to rule on the justice of a law as well as on a person's guilt or innocence. (In the United States, this is called jury nullification.) Do you support this principle? Why?

John and Elizabeth Lilburne and William Penn believed that to worship God is to love God. They believed that love could only be given freely. Do you agree? Why?

GIFT 22, pp. 79–88

Why did John Locke and the American rebels think that having a voice in what happened to their property (their taxes) was so important? What strength and freedom did possessing property give them?

Brits and Americans believed that government must be based on the popular consent of the people. It was not an idea that had previously gripped the world's imagination. Why did they want representative government? Why would you?

What inspired George Washington to join the Revolution and what kept him going through years of defeat?

What were the keys to American success? Luck? Dedication? Providence? A people who were in excellent physical shape? Generalship? The help of foreign allies? The inspiration of English freedom? George Washington's leadership?

The US Declaration of Independence states that *Whenever any government becomes destructive of our rights and liberties, we have the right to alter or abolish it.* Do you agree?

GIFT 23, pp. 89–92

We are nourished by a constitution that recognizes that freedom is our birthright. We take strength and stability from our local government 'roots', from a supporting 'trunk' of just laws and from three balanced 'branches' of government—the judiciary, executive and legislature. What happens if a branch grows too powerful? What happens if powerful people in government decide that the people are not free by natural or God-given right but only if their government allows them to be free? Why did the people of the young United States of America think the size and power of the federal government had to be limited?

GIFT 24, pp. 92–95

What meaning does the Bill of Rights have for you personally? What do you consider your most important right? Do you believe you have the right to defend yourself or your family?

GIFT 25, pp. 96–102

Why would slavery be terrible for the slave owner as well as the slave? Do people treat you as an equal? Is there anyone who doesn't? Do you feel less than equal to others at times? Why?

How do you play fair? What do you think is the difference between equality of opportunity and equality of outcome? Is it possible to have equal outcomes? Would those outcomes be financial? Emotional satisfaction? Praise? Looking at a 20th century experiment in equality of outcome—the Soviet Union—what do you think of the results?

GIFT 26, pp. 103–111

Who created the free economy?

Are ethics essential to the success of a free economy? Is the Golden Rule?

What is the connection between just law, lack of corruption, investment and jobs?

In your opinion, what is good work?

Globalization began with worldwide exploration and trade. What are the negative effects and positive contributions of globalization?

What characteristics of the free economy have lifted hundreds of millions of people out of poverty?

GIFT 27, p. 112

How have you experienced the Golden Rule in your life?

Have the teachings of Jesus influenced your life? If so, how?

NEVER FORGET, pp. 113–117

What have the gifts created for you or helped you to create?

Is it possible that the gifts are the most practical, effective and ethical way to create social justice?

Is there any reason to believe that relinquishing freedom and the creative energy of free people would help us to tackle large problems?

Do you think love was involved in the creation of the gifts?

There are people in the world struggling to defend the Inheritance that belongs to all of us. Some of them are dying as you read this paragraph. How can we—adults and children—defend the Inheritance?

Key Dates in the Book

4500–1500 BC
Megalithic people identify solar and lunar events

1st century BC–AD 1st century
Britons resist Roman conquest
Birth of Jesus Christ

Early 4th century
St Alban

5th–6th centuries
Irish share Christian teachings of compassion, forgiveness, freedom, truth and peace

9th century
Alfred the Great establishes Common Law

973
Coronation Oath affirmed covenant between leader and people

1100
Charter of Liberties

1102
Slavery outlawed in England

1166
Assize of Clarendon

1215
Magna Carta

1217
Forest Law

1265
First elected Parliament

13th century
Science in Britain becomes evidence-based

1320
Declaration of Arbroath

1381
Great Rising

1588
Defeat of Spanish Armada

1628
Petition of Right

1641
End of the Star Chamber; right to silence affirmed

1642–1651
English Civil War

1670
Juries can refuse to convict, and do not have to explain themselves

1682
Pennsylvania constitution protects religious freedom

1688/1689
British Bill of Rights

1775–1783
American Revolution

1776
Adam Smith describes free economy in Wealth of Nations

1787
U.S. Constitution

1791
U.S Bill of Rights

1805–1815
Invasion averted, Napoleon's Empire defeated

1807
Slave trade abolished in British Empire

1824
Combination Act repealed

1831
Friendly Societies formed

1833
Slavery abolished in British Empire

1846
Corn Laws repealed

1861–1865
U.S. Civil War

1868
14th Amendment to U.S. Constitution

1893/1898/1918/1920
Women win right to vote in national elections in New Zealand, Australia, Britain and U.S.

1939–1945
Defeat of Axis Powers

1989–1990s
End of Socialist tyrannies in Eastern Europe

21st century
Defending the Inheritance

Notes

Cover

Composite Image by Christine Ambrose:

Oak tree ©iStockphoto.com/Graeme Purdy

Ring of Covenant Composite
    by Christine Ambrose
Sea at Saunton ©David Abbott

Radcliffe Camera, Oxford,
    ©iStockphoto.com/Ian R Jones

DNA ©iStockphoto.com/Mads Abildgaard

The Days of Creation ('The Second Day', detail)
by Edward Burne-Jones (c. 1870), Collection of
the Fogg Art Museum, Harvard University

George Washington Composite
    by Christine Ambrose
Washington on Rushmore
    ©iStockphoto.com/William Blacke

Alfred the Great Composite
    by Christine Ambrose
Statue of Alfred by Count Gleichen (1877)
©iStockphoto.com/The Biggles
Background from the Lindisfarne Gospels
(7th-8th century), Collection of the British
Library, London

Page ii

Acorn & Tree Composite Image
    by Christine Ambrose

Page iii

We must recognise..., Winston Churchill
(Théâtre des Ambassadeurs, Paris: 24 September 1936); text from Winston S. Churchill,
*Never Give In! The Best of Winston Churchill's
Speeches* (Hyperion: 2003)

Page vi

Big Ben by Simon Taylor, phooto.co.uk, (GNU
Free Documentation License & Creative
Commons Attribution ShareAlike 3.0 License:
commons.wikimedia.org/wiki/Commons:
GNU_Free_Documentation_License and
creativecommons.org/licenses/by-sa/3.0/)

Page vii

Big Ben, St Stephen's Tower, Westminster, by
AWN Pugin, completed in 1852; photo (detail)
©iStockphoto.com/Ian Tatlock

Page ix

Golden tree ©iStockphoto.com/Roberto
Sanchez

Page xii

A man who knows..., Oscar Wilde, *Lady
Windemere's Fan* (1892)

Cartoon by Lena Lenček

Page 1

Stonehenge Composite Image
    by Christine Ambrose

I am a part..., Alfred Lord Tennyson,
"Ulysses" (1833; published 1842)

Page 2

Megalithic people sailed..., a point supported by
Francis Pryor, *Britain BC* (HarperCollins UK:
2003)

There is evidence that the Golden Ratio..., an idea
developed by Vivian Linacre, *The General Rule:
A Guide to Customary Weights and Measures*
(Squeeze Press: 2007)

Ring of Brodgar
©iStockphoto.com/David Woods

Astronomical clocks..., an hypothesis explored by
Sir Joseph Norman Lockyer, *Stonehenge and Other
British Stone Monuments Astronomically Considered*
(Macmillan: 1906), and by Professor of Engineering Science Alexander Thom, *Megalithic
Lunar Observatories* (Oxford: 1971)

Page 3

Acorn Composite Image by Christine Ambrose

What I saw far surpassed..., Osbert Crawford
quoted by John Julius Norwich, *Britain's Heritage*
(Continuum Publishing: 1983)

Page 4

Boy ©iStockphoto.com/Agata Malchrowicz

Hill and Torc Composite Image
by Christine Ambrose
Eggardon Hill, Dorset ©iStockphoto.com/
Black Beck Photographic
Great Torc, Snettisham Hoard,
Collection of the British Museum

Page 5

The words free and friend..., Oxford English Dictionary
(Oxford University Press: 1989)

Roman legion re-enactment
©iStockphoto.com/standby

Young girl ©iStockphoto.com/kerher

By 1000 BC..., a time frame supported by Steven
Oppenheimer, *The Origins of the British* (Basic
Books: 2006)

Page 6

Remember, officers and soldiers..., George Washington (General Orders: 23 August 1776)

Eleutheria..., Aeschylus, *The Persians* (472 BC)

The Romans make a wasteland..., Calgacus quoted
by Tacitus, *Agricola* (AD 98)

The next day, an awful silence..., Tacitus, *Agricola*
(AD 98)

Hadrian's Wall Composite Image
by Christine Ambrose
Hadrian's Wall ©iStockphoto.com/BMPix

Page 7

Bombed children in London, U.S. National
Archives 306-NT-3163V

Hands Composite Image
by Christine Ambrose
Hands ©iStockphoto.com/Don Bayley

Page 8

Evil is..., Richard Fernandez, "Which was made
of brass" (pajamasmedia.com: November 2008)

Some people want..., Socrates quoted by Plato,
Lysis (c. 380 BC)

Lovers are..., CS Lewis, *The Four Loves*
(Harcourt, Brace: 1960)

In the Roman city of Verulamium...,
Roman practices are described by Alison Taylor
in "Burial with the Romans" (British Archaeol-
ogy: March 2003)

There is a disease..., attributed to Aeschylus,
Prometheus Bound (5th century BC)

I worship and adore..., St Alban quoted by the
Venerable Bede, *The Ecclesiastical History of the
English People* (c. 731)

Page 9

Cathedral of St Alban
©iStockphoto.com/Stuart R Taylor

Within every human person..., George Weigel,
*Against the Grain: Christianity and Democracy,
War and Peace* (Crossroad Publishing: 2008)

Greater love..., Jesus quoted in the Gospel of
John (c. AD 90)

Page 10

I wonder if we realize..., George VI in his last
radio broadcast to the British people
(Christmas, 1951)

Boy ©iStockphoto.com/Rob Friedman

Page 11

St Patrick's *Confessio* (c. 450) describes his misery as a slave and his escape.

They built a community..., described by Robert
Van de Weyer, *Celtic Gifts* (Canterbury Press:
1997)

Iona ©iStockphoto.com/Iain Sarjeant

After the fall of Rome..., Hugh Johnson, *Wine*
(Thomas Nelson: 1966)

Swan ©iStockphoto.com/Jostein Hauge

But now they drift..., William Butler Yeats,
"The Wild Swans at Coole" (1919)

Page 12

Iona Cloisters
©iStockphoto.com/Iain Sarjeant

Translucent source..., Robert Van de Weyer, *Celtic
Gifts* (Canterbury Press: 1997)

Gold belt buckle, Sutton Hoo ship-burial
(AD 7th century), Collection of the British
Museum

Page 13

Celtic Cross at Bolton Abbey, Northumbria (Yorkshire) ©iStockphoto.com/mikeuk

The growth of personality..., Roger Scruton, *England, An Elegy* (Chatto & Windus: 2000)

Rooted in love..., The Venerable Bede, *The Ecclesiastical History of the English People* (c. 731)

Page 14

Psalm 89, the Book of Psalms (10th century BC)

Do a miracle, A Celtic Miscellany (Routledge & Kegan Paul: 1951; Penguin Classics: 1971)

Christ and Landscape
Composite Image by Christine Ambrose
Christ Pantocrator Icon (c. 6th century), St Catherine's Monastery, Sinai
The Forest of Dean ©iStockphoto.com/GELL

Out of the Carpenter's shop..., Oscar Wilde, *De Profundis* (Methuen: 1905)

Page 15

Who is my mother..., Jesus quoted in the Gospels of Matthew (c. AD 60-80), Mark (c. AD 50-67) and Luke (c. AD 37-61)

Who did sin? Gospel of John (c. AD 90)

Your words are fair..., John Richard Green, *A Short History of the English People*, Vol. I (Harper & Brothers: 1893)

Snowdrops ©iStockphoto.com/Anettelinnea

Page 16

An intellectual asked..., Jesus quoted in the Gospels of Luke (c. AD 37-61), Matthew (c. AD 60-80) and Mark (c. AD 50-67)

Blessed are..., Jesus quoted in the Gospel of Matthew (c. AD 60-80)

God loves..., paraphrase of Anne Lamott, *Traveling Mercies* (Pantheon Books: 1999)

No one lives..., Jesus quoted in the Gospels of Matthew (c. AD 60-80) and Luke (c. AD 37-61)

Children ©iStockphoto.com/Rosemarie Gearhart

Page 17

How many times..., Gospel of Matthew (c. AD 60-80)

Forgiveness was a concept..., paraphrase of Hannah Arendt, *The Human Condition* (University of Chicago Press: 1958)

Rainbow ©iStockphoto.com/Julian Barkway

Pay to Caesar..., Jesus quoted in the Gospels of Matthew (c. AD 60-80), Mark (c. AD 50-67) and Luke (c. AD 37-61)

The kingdom of God..., Jesus quoted in the Gospel of Luke (c. AD 37-61)

He has sent me..., the Prophet Isaiah, the Book of Isaiah (c. 742 BC), and the Gospel of Luke (c. AD 37-61)

Our Lord..., paraphrase of Julian of Norwich, *Revelations of Divine Love* (c. 1373)

Page 18

For this I came..., Jesus quoted in the Gospel of John (c. AD 90)

Thy kingdom come..., Jesus quoted in the Gospels of Matthew (c. AD 60-80) and Luke (c. AD 37-61)

...receive the Holy Spirit..., Jesus quoted in the Gospel of John (c. AD 90)

A man's life..., the Venerable Bede, *The Ecclesiastical History of the English People* (c. 731)

The Days of Creation ('The Second Day', detail) by Edward Burne-Jones (c. 1870), Collection of the Fogg Art Museum, Harvard University

Page 19

Look, I'm at the door..., Jesus quoted in the Book of Revelation (c. AD 81-95)

The greatest gift..., Dante, *The Divine Comedy*, "Paradiso" (c. 1320)

The original meaning..., Oxford English Dictionary (Oxford University Press: 1989)

Page 20

Girl on beach ©iStockphoto.com/ximagination

Bear in mind..., Socrates to the judges who had condemned him to death, quoted by Plato, *The Apology* (c. 390 BC) translated by Harold North Fowler (Harvard University Press: 1914)

Athenian Herm, detail (c. 440 BC) Roman copy, Collection of the Metropolitan Museum of Art, New York. Image ©2005 TPB, Esq. (unbillablehours.typepad.com)

Page 21

Watchers and stars
©iStockphoto.com/digipixpro

Page 22

Book on glass ©iStockphoto.com/Nadezda Firsova

Character matters enormously..., Thomas Sowell, "'Non-Judgmental' Nonsense" (townhall.com: March 2008)

Anglo-Saxon protection of individual property rights was described by Montesquieu in *The Spirit of the Laws* (1748) and by Alan Macfarlane in *Origins of English Individualism* (Wiley-Blackwell: 1979).

All that is gold does not glitter..., JRR Tolkien, *The Fellowship of the Ring* (George Allen & Unwin: 1954)

Page 23

Viking ship
©iStockphoto.com/Andrzej Tokarski

I remember how..., King Alfred, his preface to the *Cura Pastoralis* of Pope Gregory I (c. 887)

Page 24

Cartoon by Lena Lenček

Alfred the Great Composite Image
by Christine Ambrose
Statue of Alfred in Winchester by Hamo Thornycroft (1901) ©iStockphoto.com/Andy Hill

Page 25

They fought for their God-given..., Emily Hickey, *Our Catholic Heritage in English Literature of Pre-Conquest Days* (Sands & Company: 1910)

Page 27

Alfred Composite Image
by Christine Ambrose
Statue of Alfred by Count Gleichen (1877)
©iStockphoto.com/The Biggles
Background from the Lindisfarne Gospels (7th-8th century), Collection of the British Library, London

Page 28

Do not murder..., Jesus quoted in the Gospels of Matthew (c. AD 60-80) and Mark (c. AD 50-67). The quotations vary slightly.

Proverbs, Book of Proverbs (10th century BC)

Page 29

Glastonbury Tor and St Michael's Tower
©iStockphoto.com/Matt Collingwood

They shall build up..., the Prophet Isaiah, Isaiah (c. 742 BC)

Page 30

You know that..., Jesus quoted in the Gospel of Luke (c. AD 37-61). He makes a similar statement in the Gospel of Matthew (c. AD 60-80)

Harp ©iStockphoto.com/Scott Slattery

Page 31

Ring of Covenant Composite Image
by Christine Ambrose
Sea at Saunton ©David Abbott

A promise is..., a slight paraphrase of *The choice of a form is...*, Wendell Berry, *Standing by Words* (North Point Press: 1983)

Page 32

Stone mason, drawing by unknown artist (11th century), *Ms. Cott. Claud. B iv*, John Richard Green, *A Short History of the English People*, Vol. I (Harper & Brothers: 1893)

Tower of London Chapel, John Richard Green, *A Short History of the English People*, Vol. I (Harper & Brothers: 1893)

Page 33

Fiction of tenure..., William Blackstone, *Commentaries on the Laws of England* (1765-1769)

The New Forest ©iStockphoto.com/Joe Gough

Uneasy lies the head..., William Shakespeare, *Henry IV, Part II* (c. 1598)

Page 34

Truth is justice..., Anselm, *On Truth* (c. 1070)

Was elected king..., William of Malmesbury, *Chronicles of the Kings of England* (c. 1120)

Henry I ©iStockphoto.com/Duncan Walker

Page 35

Uneducated king..., Medieval proverb

Woman ©iStockphoto.com/knape

I wore the veil trembling..., John Richard Green, *A Short History of the English People*, Vol. I (Harper & Brothers: 1893)

Page 36

Sun and trees ©iStockphoto.com/Todd Smith

We needed to stop asking..., Viktor Frankl, *Man's Search for Meaning* (Washington Square Press: 1959)

Boy ©iStockphoto.com/tillsonburg

Young men..., William of Malmesbury, *Chronicles of the Kings of England* (c. 1120)

Page 37

The Westminster Council also addressed the celibacy of priests.

Windsor Tower ©iStockphoto.com/Jon Helgason

Page 38

Riders ©iStockphoto.com/Dawn Hudson

Knight, drawing by unknown artist (13th century), *MS. Roy. 2. A. xxii*, John Richard Green, *A Short History of the English People*, Vol. I (Harper & Brothers: 1893)

Page 39

William Marshal's life, *L'Histoire de Guillaume le Maréchal* (13th century) and *The Oxford Dictionary of National Biography* (oxforddnb.com)

Belt your waist..., Paul, Letter to the Ephesians (c. AD 58-63)

Page 40

Ste Jeanne d'Arc (c.1485), Centre Historique des Archives Nationales, Paris

Quest for the Holy Grail, "The Arming & Departure of the Knights", tapestry by Edward Burne-Jones, William Morris and John Henry Dearle (c. 1890), Collection of the Birmingham Museum & Art Gallery

Page 41

Field and animals ©iStockphoto.com/Brett Charlton

Women traders..., *The Oxford Dictionary of National Biography* (oxforddnb.com)

If..., Rudyard Kipling, "If" (1895/1910)

Page 42

Wilton Diptych (detail) by an unknown artist (c. 1395), Collection of the National Gallery, London

Seal of Robert Fitzwalter, John Richard Green, *A Short History of the English People*, Vol. I (Harper & Brothers: 1893)

Page 43

Dragon of Wales ©iStockphoto.com/Duncan Walker

William Marshal on his tomb, John Richard Green, *A Short History of the English People*, Vol. I (Harper & Brothers: 1893)

Page 44

It is for liberty..., Letter to the Galatians (c. AD 54)

Star ©iStockphoto.com/mammuth

Page 45

Driving the flagitious..., William of Malmesbury, *Chronicles of the Kings of England* (c. 1120)

Bury St Edmunds Bridge (as it appeared in the 13th century), John Richard Green, *A Short History of the English People*, Vol. I (Harper & Brothers: 1893)

Wycoller Bridge © Howard Maunders (beautifulbritain.co.uk)

Page 46

In an environment..., Kathryn Jean Lopez (*National Review online*: July 2008)

After they had discoursed..., Roger of Wendover, *Flores Historiarum* (c. 1225). Contemporary sources, including *Chronique de l'Histoire des Ducs de Normandie*, support his account.

Temple Church ©iStockphoto.com/Peter Spiro

Page 47

Men talking, drawing by an unknown artist (11th century), John Richard Green, *A Short History of the English People*, Vol. I (Harper & Brothers: 1893)

Page 48

Map of 13th century London, W.J. Loftie, *A History of London* (E. Stanford: 1884) Hand-coloured by Christine Ambrose

Page 49

To no one... Composite Image by Christine Ambrose

Page 51

Family ©iStockphoto.com/Andresr

Page 52

Rochester Castle ©iStockphoto.com/Nicholas Mosienko

Red deer ©iStockphoto.com/Richard Bowden

Page 53

Forest ©iStockphoto.com/AVTG

The iniquities of the royal forest..., Danny Danziger & John Gillingham, *1215, the Year of Magna Carta* (Hodder and Stoughton: 2003)

Page 54

Kenilworth Castle & Bachelor Knights Composite Image by Christine Ambrose Kenilworth Castle by JD Forrester (GNU Free Documentation License & Creative Commons Attribution ShareAlike 3.0 License: commons. wikimedia.org/wiki/Commons:GNU_Free_ Documentation_License and creativecommons. org/licenses/by-sa/3.0/)

If a nation values..., W. Somerset Maugham, *Strictly Personal* (Doubleday, Doran: 1941)

Page 55

Court of Henry III, probably by Matthew Paris (13th century) MS. *Cott. Nero D. i*, John Richard Green, *A Short History of the English People*, Vol. I (Harper & Brothers: 1893)

Seal of Oxford, *Ingram Memorials of Oxford*, John Richard Green, *A Short History of the English People*, Vol. I (Harper & Brothers: 1893)

Page 56

Cartoon by Lena Lenček

Imbued with the ideal..., "Simon de Montfort", *The Oxford Dictionary of National Biography* (oxforddnb.com)

Gnawed and tunneled..., Edith Pargeter, *The Brothers of Gwynedd* (Headline: 1989)

Page 57

Lewes Castle ©iStockphoto.com/Ian Hamilton

Page 58

Weighing vegetables ©iStockphoto.com/Sean Locke

Governments that are answerable..., Bret Stephens (*Wall Street Journal*: 30 September 2009)

Page 59

They have our bodies..., Histories have reported Montfort's words differently. This version seemed correct to us.

Vale of Evesham ©iStockphoto.com/Andre Maritz

Unless a grain..., Jesus quoted in the Gospel of John (c. AD 90)

Page 60

Parliament ©iStockphoto.com/DHuss

Page 61

Comet Hale Bopp ©iStockphoto.com/Michael Puerzer

Page 62

Virtue does not come..., and *I do not think I know...*, Socrates quoted in Plato's *Apology*, adapted from the translation by Harold North Fowler (Harvard University Press: 1914...1999)

Baby with I-V
©iStockphoto.com/zoomstudio.pl

Page 63

Availability bias..., Daniel Kahneman was awarded a Nobel Prize in Economics (2002) for his work, in collaboration with Amos Tversky, on how people make decisions.

Man shaving
©iStockphoto.com/Randolph Pamphrey

Boy on beach ©iStockphoto.com/Lee Foster

If I have seen further..., Isaac Newton to Robert Hooke (1676)

Get the Facts..., Dr Thomas Fuller, *Gnomologia* (1732)

Page 64

Seek information..., Jason Zweig, "Ignoring the Yes-Man in Your Head" (*Wall Street Journal*: November 2009)

Teenagers
©iStockphoto.com/Lise Gagne

Elephant Island ©iStockphoto.com/brytta

Page 65

All Souls College Oxford
©iStockphoto.com/Anthony Dodd

Biotechnology could be..., Freeman Dyson (*New York Review of Books*: 12 June 2008)

Page 66

Radcliffe Camera
©iStockphoto.com/Ian R Jones

Cartoon by Lena Lenček

Cambridge Quad
©iStockphoto.com/Burcin Tuncer

Page 67

St. Bartholomew's Hospital by Nevilley (GNU Free Documentation License & Creative Commons Attribution ShareAlike 3.0 License: commons.wikimedia.org/wiki/Commons: GNU_Free_Documentation_License and creativecommons.org/licenses/by-sa/3.0/)

Sackville College (Tuileries Brochures: 1930)

Page 68

Hands ©iStockphoto.com/hidesy

Page 69

I was an honest..., Alice Driver quoted by John Foxe, *Booke of Martyrs* (1563)

Child and candles
©iStockphoto.com/Franky De Meyer

The bright red thread..., Michael Novak, *On Two Wings, Humble Faith and Common Sense at the American Founding* (Encounter Books: 2002)

Boy and pigs (detail) (1950s) Courtesy of the Museum of English Rural Life, University of Reading

Page 70

And Jesus..., Gospel of Matthew (c. AD 60-80)

Girl
©iStockphoto.com/Jose Antonio Sánchez Reyes

Page 71

John Hampden, *The Rise of Democracy* (Project Gutenberg eText 19609 & Wikimedia Commons)

Gold Coin of Charles I (1643), John Richard Green, *A Short History of the English People*, Vol. III (Harper & Brothers: 1893)

Newgate Prison (1684), John Richard Green, *A Short History of the English People*, Vol. III (Harper & Brothers: 1893)

Page 72

Aberdeen Lighthouse
©iStockphoto.com/Mike Bentley

Robert the Bruce and William Wallace Memorial
©iStockphoto.com/fotoVoyager

Page 73

I have a right..., John Lilburne, before a committee of the House of Commons (1645)

Father and son ©iStockphoto.com/Lise Gagne

The rights of man come..., U.S. President John F. Kennedy, Inaugural Address (1961)

Page 74

All men and women..., John Lilburne,
Free Man's Freedom Vindicated (1647)

Torch (detail) ©iStockphoto.com/James Steidl

Page 75

Ye are Englishmen..., William Penn, transcript of
trial (1670)

Izaak Walton Window, Winchester Cathedral,
the gift of the fishermen of England and
America

Page 76

Juries have a right..., Paraphrase of John Jay (U.S.
Supreme Court, Georgia v. Brailsford 1794)

I consider trial by jury..., Thomas Jefferson writing
to Thomas Paine (1789)

Page 77

Pennsylvania ©iStockphoto.com/Pgiam

Soul liberty..., phrase coined by Roger Williams,
founder of Rhode Island

Life is short..., Henri-Frédéric Amiel, *Journal
Intime* (1868; published 1882)

Page 78

Penn State elms
©iStockphoto.com/Mark Steinruck

Page 79

Boston Tea Party lithograph
Nathaniel Currier (1846)

Page 80

United Kingdom £2 Coin celebrating the Ter-
centenary of the British Bill of Rights (1989)

The Glorious Revolution inspired..., a theory sup-
ported by Michael Barone in *Our First Revolution:
The Remarkable British Upheaval that Inspired
America's Founding Fathers* (Crown: 2007)

We are born to the bright..., New Yorkers to the
Lord Mayor & City of London (May 1775)

The Parliament of..., George Washington, letter
to George William Fairfax (July 1774)

Page 81

Virginia House of Burgesses, Williamsburg
©iStockphoto.com/Vanessa Goodrich

John Locke by Herman Verelst (c. 1685),
Collection of the National Portrait Gallery, London

Page 82

I know not what course..., Patrick Henry to the
Virginia Convention (March 1775)

Lexington Minute Man, Captain John Parker
by Henry Hudson Kitson (1900) Photo by
Daderot (GNU Free Documentation License &
Creative Commons Attribution ShareAlike 3.0
License: commons.wikimedia.org/wiki/Com-
mons:GNU_Free_Documentation_License and
creativecommons.org/licenses/by-sa/3.0/)

Page 83

Washington by Gutzon Borglum (1934)
©iStockphoto.com/Paul Fries

Washington dispenses..., Maj. General Henry
Knox to his wife (1775), Parry, Allison &
Skousen, *The Real George Washington* (National
Center for Constitutional Studies: 1991)

I shall constantly bear..., George Washington to
Congress (1783)

Page 84

It is hard to make government..., GK Chesterton
(*Illustrated London News*: August 1918)

Cartoon by Lena Lenček

*Presenting the Draft of the Declaration of Indepen-
dence to the Second Continental Congress* by John
Trumbull (1817-1819), US Capitol rotunda

Page 85

These are the times, Thomas Paine, *The American
Crisis* (1776)

Nation Makers (at the Battle of Brandywine) by
Howard Pyle (1903), Collection of the Brandywine River Museum

The Americans are the sons... William Pitt, later
Lord Chatham (Speech to House of Commons:
16 January 1776)

Page 86

I will not..., George Washington to New Jersey Governor William Livingston (November 1776), Parry, Allison & Skousen, *The Real George Washington* (National Center for Constitutional Studies: 1991)

Prayer at Valley Forge (detail) by Henry Brueckner (1866)

Valley Forge ©iStockphoto.com/Aimin Tang

That host of infamous..., George Washington (1779) Parry, Allison & Skousen, *The Real George Washington* (National Center for Constitutional Studies: 1991)

Labyrinthine hell..., Robert Leckie, *The Wars of America* (Harper & Row: 1968)

There are conflicting reports on the numbers of British and American troops at the Battle of Brandywine. The consensus: almost 30,000 with Americans outnumbered.

Page 87

It was not pleasant..., Major Patrick Ferguson (Edinburgh University Library Records: 1778)

Prayer at Valley Forge (detail) by Henry Brueckner (1866)

No man has a more..., George Washington to the Rev. William Gordon (1776) Parry, Allison & Skousen, *The Real George Washington* (National Center for Constitutional Studies: 1991)

Page 88

It is assuredly better to go laughing..., George Washington to Theodrick Bland (1786) Parry, Allison & Skousen, *The Real George Washington* (National Center for Constitutional Studies: 1991)

Statue of Liberty and boy ©iStockphoto.com/cristiani

Yorktown stamp, U.S. Postal Service ©iStockphoto.com/Ray Roper

Page 89

Independence Hall Composite Image by Christine Ambrose

Shaken to its foundation..., George Washington to Thomas Jefferson (1787) Parry, Allison & Skousen, *The Real George Washington* (National Center for Constitutional Studies: 1991)

The greatest fabric..., John Adams quoted by David McCullough, *John Adams* (Simon and Schuster: 2002)

Page 90

Freedom of speech..., (National Post: 15 April 2010)

Page 91

We the People ©iStockphoto.com/DNY59

Power was balanced..., Parry, Allison & Skousen, *The Real George Washington* (National Center for Constitutional Studies: 1991)

Oak Leaves and Acorns by Susan Muther

Page 92

A nation may establish..., Alexis de Tocqueville, Democracy in America, Vol. 1, (1835); translated by Henry Reeve (D. Appleton: 1904)

Mozart ©iStockphoto.com/wrangle

Congress does not have..., Thomas Jefferson to Albert Gallatin (1817)

Page 93

Man with gun and dog ©iStockphoto.com/Stuart Blyth

The right of citizens to bear arms..., US Senator Hubert H. Humphrey (*Guns Magazine*, 1960)

The right of self-defense, St. George Tucker, *Blackstone's commentaries on the Laws of England: with notes of reference to the constitution and laws of the federal government of the United States, and of the Commonwealth of Virginia* (1803)

Both oligarch and tyrant..., Aristotle, *Politics* (c. 350 BC)

Why do you think they disarmed..., attributed to Thomas Sowell (Townhall.com)

Page 96

Man with book ©iStockphoto.com/Christine Glade

I have a dream..., Martin Luther King (Lincoln Memorial, Washington DC: 28 August 1963)

Page 97

Let us not pray..., Abraham Lincoln quoted by Francis Carpenter, *Six Months in the White House with Abraham Lincoln* (1864)

Portrait of Olaudah Equiano (18th century; attribution debated), Collection of the Royal Albert Memorial Museum, Exeter

Surely this traffic..., Olaudah Equiano, *The Interesting Narrative or Life of Olaudah Equiano* (1789)

HMS *Black Joke* by Nicholas Matthews Condy (c. 1840), Collection of the Royal Naval Museum, Greenwich

Page 98

The Sharp Family by Johann Zoffany (c. 1779), Collection of the National Portrait Gallery, London

Girl meditating
©iStockphoto.com/GhostOfTragedy

Boudicca Composite Image by Christine Ambrose
Boudicca and her daughters by Thomas Thornycroft (1902)
Boudicca ©iStockphoto.com/vladimir.org

Page 99

The Armada Portrait, Elizabeth I, by George Gower (1588), Collection of Woburn Abbey

Portrait of A Lady by John Russell, RA (18th century), Christie's Images Ltd

It is our choices..., JK Rowling, *Harry Potter and the Chamber of Secrets* (Arthur A. Levine Books: 1999)

Page 100

Florence Nightingale at Scutari Hospital (c. 1855) ©iStockphoto.com/Hulton

Mary Seacole by Albert Charles Challen (c. 1869), Collection of the National Portrait Gallery, London

Emmeline Pankhurst (1913), U.S. Library of Congress

Page 101

Edith Cavell (c. 1900)

Margaret Thatcher (1980s) provided by Chris Collins, the Margaret Thatcher Foundation (Creative Commons Attribution-ShareAlike 3.0 License; creativecommons.org/licenses/by-sa/3.0/)

Girl reading
©iStockphoto.com/Carmen Martínez Banús

The long-term benefits..., Paul E. Peterson (Wall Street Journal: 16 March 2010) explaining how school choice improved student performance in 29 industrialized countries according to a Harvard University study

Page 102

Rugby player ©iStockphoto.com/Mark Kolbe

Be that..., Shakespeare, *Twelfth Night or What You Will* (c.1600)

Canadian children ©iStockphoto.com/Honuart

Page 103

Earth and Sun ©iStockphoto.com/narvikk

The myth of power, Gregory Bateson, *Steps to an Ecology of Mind* (University of Chicago Press: 1972) and Friedrich Hayek, *Individualism and Economic Order* (Routledge and Kegan Paul: 1949)

Page 104

Globe Theatre ©iStockphoto.com/Lance Bellers

Fishing harbour ©iStockphoto.com/fotoVoyager
Elinor Ostrom won the 2009 Nobel Prize for Economics by establishing that local citizens often do a far superior job of managing shared common resources such as fishing grounds than government does.

Child painting
©iStockphoto.com/Carmen Martínez Banús

The famous yellow pencil..., Leonard E Reed "I, Pencil: My Family Tree as told to Leonard E. Read" (*The Freeman*: 1958) made famous by Milton and Rose Friedman in *Free to Choose*

Page 105

Watcher ©iStockphoto.com/AccesscodeHFM

The free economy has lifted hundreds of millions..., Carl Schramm (realclearmarkets.com 21 May 2009) *In the touchstone year of 1820, 84% of the world's population lived in what would today be judged 'extreme poverty'. ...According to the World Bank, in the last 30 years alone, the number of people living in extreme poverty fell by 25%, or 500 million people.*

Adam Smith, South Western University of Finance and Economics, Chengdu, China. Photo permission by Tom G Palmer (tomgpalmer.com) of the Cato Institute (cato.org/) and the Atlas Economic Research Foundation (tom.palmer@atlasnetwork.org)

Some work preserves..., Wendell Berry, *Standing by Words* (North Point Press: 1983)

Page 106

Prior to capitalism..., Walter E Williams "Capitalism and the Common Man" (George Mason University: January 2000)

Vancouver, BC ©iStockphoto.com/Natalia Bratslavsky

Canterbury Pilgrims by William Blake (c. 1820), Collection of Northwestern University Library

Messengers carrying letters..., *The Oxford Illustrated History of Medieval England* (Oxford University Press: 2001)

They eat plentifully..., The point is made by Alan Macfarlane, *Origins of English Individualism* (Wiley-Blackwell: 1979)

Page 107

An evolutionary process..., Steve Conover, "Letters to the Editor" (*Wall Street Journal*: January 2010)

Astonishing phenomenon..., James Bartholomew, *The Welfare State We're In* (Methuen Publishing: 2004)

Almost the entire social order..., Roger Scruton, *England, An Elegy* (Chatto & Windus: 2000)

African woman and child ©iStockphoto.com/ alaincouillaud

If the industrial nations..., James Shikwati, "For God's Sake, Please Stop the Aid" (*Spiegel Online International*: 4 July 2005)

If people are neighborly..., Glenn Reynolds (pajamasmedia.com/instapundit/ 27 September 2009)

Page 108

Chairing the Member by William Hogarth (c. 1754), Collection of Sir John Soane's Museum, London

"Taxman" by George Harrison, The Beatles, *Revolver* (1966)

Power tends to corrupt, and absolute power corrupts absolutely, Lord Acton to Bishop Mandell Creighton (1887)

Lady Godiva ©iStockphoto.com/forgiss

Backed by a violent foreign state..., This was Soviet Russia's advance into Europe. *An iron curtain has descended across the Continent*, Winston Churchill warned in 1946 in Fulton, Missouri.

Page 109

Prague silhouette ©iStockphoto.com/S. Greg Panosian

Paul Revere Silver Teapot, M.S. Rau Antiques, LLC, rauantiques.com

Page 110

The idea that political..., Ludwig von Mises "Laissez Faire or Dictatorship" (*Plain Talk*: January 1949, republished by the Ludwig von Mises Institute)

"The Goose and the Golden Egg" by Milo Winter, *The Aesop for Children* (Rand McNally: 1919)

Prague young people ©iStockphoto.com/mammamaart

Page 111

Anteros by Alfred Gilbert (1892) ©iStockphoto.com/track5

In this particular case..., a paraphrase, U. S. President Ronald Reagan's Inaugural Address (20 January 1981)

The advance of human liberty..., Ronald Reagan, "Tear down this wall" (Berlin: 12 June, 1987)

Cartoon by Lena Lenček

Index

Habeas corpus, 50, 76, 92
Hadrian's Wall, 6
Hampden, John, 71, 72
Harrison, George, 108
Hayek, Friedrich, 103
Henges, 1–2
Henry I, 34, 35, 36, 45
Henry II, 40, 41, 47, 53
Henry III, 52, 54–58
Henry, Patrick, 82
Hilda, 13
Hoard, Snettisham, 4
Hodgkin, Dorothy, 101
Hogarth, William, 108
Holy Grail, Quest for, 29, 40
Holy Spirit, 18
Honesty, 27–28, 30, 32, 55–56, 60, 66, 69, 72, 83, 109, 111, 112
Hong Kong, 106
Hope, 2, 16, 20, 41, 57, 77, 110, 115
Horses, 3, 8, 38, 39, 40, 59, 85; horseman, 56, 87
Hospitals, 19, 67, 98, 107
House of Representatives, US, 60
Houses of Parliament, Westminster, 60
Independence Hall, Philadelphia, 89
India, 49, 51
Industrial Revolution, 106
Iona, 11, 12
Iron Age 4, 5
Isaiah, 29
James II, 57
Jay, John, 76, 80
Jebb, Eglantyne, 100
Jefferson, Thomas, 76, 92
Jesus Christ (Isu Mac De), 9, 11–19, 28, 30, 59, 70, 112, 122
Joan of Arc (Jeanne d' Arc), 40
John (King), 38, 41–53, 54, 57
John of Salisbury, 55
Johnson, Hugh, 11
Judeo-Christian ethics, 11–20, 22, 25, 27–29, 32, 35, 39, 70, 96–97, 111, 112
Julian, Lady of Norwich, 17, 44, 99
Jury, trial by, jurors, 27, 47, 50, 73–76, 78, 80, 92, 94–95, 120
Justice, injustice, 10, 11, 14, 15, 16, 19–22, 26–28, 29, 30, 32, 33, 34, 38, 39, 42, 44–46, 49,

53, 55, 56, 67, 81, 88, 90–91, 105, 112, 116, 120
Kennedy, John Fitzgerald, 73
Kett, Robert, 91
Kidnapping, 11, 36
King, Martin Luther, 96
Kipling, Rudyard, 41
Knight(s), 38–49, 51–52, 54–60, 119
Kosciuszko, Tadeusz, 86
Lady Godiva, 108
Lady of the Mercians (Aethelflaed), 24, 98
Lafayette, Marquis de, 87–88
Lake District National Park, 117
Langton, Stephen, 44–47, 49, 51, 52
Law(s), 8, 11, 19, 20, 21–28, 31, 33, 35, 37, 44–47, 49–51, 55, 57, 58, 66, 69, 71, 73–76, 78, 80–82, 89–95, 98, 102, 105–108, 110–111, 115, 118–121, 122
Law(s), physical, 2–4, 21, 32, 62–65
Law(s), spiritual, 15, 17, 19, 20, 28, 32, 44, 112
Leadership, 26–27, 30–32, 83, 100, 119, 120
Lewis, CS, 8
Liberties, Charter of, 34–35, 45
Liberty, 6, 38, 44, 48–49, 57, 66, 69, 70, 77 (soul liberty), 79, 81–82, 88, 90–92, 95, 106, 110, 111
Lighthouse, Aberdeen, 72
Lilburne, John and Elizabeth, 68–74
Lincoln, Abraham, 97
Lindisfarne, 13
Locke, John, 81, 120
London, 7, 26, 30, 32, 41, 45, 46, 47, 48 (map), 50, 51, 58, 60, 67, 68, 69, 75, 80, 89, 103, 104, 106
Londoners, 7, 38, 48, 55, 57, 73, 74
Lopez, Kathryn Jean 46
Lord Acton, 108
Love, xi, 5, 7, 8–9, 11, 13, 14, 15–17, 20, 23, 26, 28, 29, 38, 41, 44, 55, 64, 70, 77, 79, 85, 88, 97, 99, 102, 109, 111, 112, 116, 119, 120–121, 140
Mac De, Isu (see Jesus)
Magna Carta, 38–53, 54, 58, 65, 71, 73, 90, 119, 122
Malmesbury, William of, 36, 45
Marshal, Isabel, 40–41
Marshal, William, 39–43, 47, 49, 51–52
Marshal, William, Jr., 43, 47
Martyr(s), 68–70

The people who helped to create
the Inheritance were inspired by the
'Love that moves the sun and the other stars',
by the desire for freedom and the thrill of exploration,
by dire necessity and common sense,
by creativity and compassion.